The
Puritan Dilemma

Edmund S. Morgan

The
Puritan Dilemma

The Story of John Winthrop

Second Edition

Series Editor Oscar Handlin

 LONGMAN

An imprint of Addison Wesley Longman, Inc.

New York • Reading, Massachusetts • Menlo Park, California • Harlow, England
Don Mills, Ontario • Sydney • Mexico City • Madrid • Amsterdam

Acquisitions Editor: Jay O'Callaghan
Developmental Editor: Jen McCaffery
Executive Marketing Manager: Sue Westmoreland
Project Manager: Donna DeBenedictis
Production Intern: Amy Lipman
Design Manager/Text Designer: John Callahan
Cover Designer: Kay Petronio
Cover/Frontispiece Photo: Courtesy, American Antiquarian Society
Prepress Services Supervisor: Valerie A. Vargas
Electronic Production Specialist/Electronic Page Makeup: Joanne Del Ben
Senior Print Buyer: Hugh Crawford
Printer and Binder: RR Donnelley & Sons Company
Cover Printer: The Lehigh Press, Inc.

Library of Congress Cataloging-in-Publication Data
Morgan, Edmund Sears.
   The Puritan dilemma: the story of John Winthrop/edited by Oscar
Handlin.—2nd ed.
     p.   cm.—(The library of American biography)
   Includes bibliographical references and index.
   ISBN 0-321-04369-3 (pbk.)
   1. Winthrop, John, 1588-1649. 2. Governors—Massachusetts—Biography.
3. Puritans—Massachusetts—Biography. 4. Massachusetts—History—Colonial
period, ca. 1600–1775. 5. Puritans—Massachusetts—History—17th century.
I. Handlin, Oscar, 1915–   . II. Title. III. Series.
F67.W79M66   1999
974.4'02'092—dc21
[B]   98-35269
                                                                                      CIP

Please visit our website at http://longman.awl.com

ISBN 0-321-04369-3

   13 14 15 16 DOC 09 08 07 06 05

For
my mother

Contents

Editor's Preface

From its first discovery, the emptiness of the New World made it the field for social experiment. Crowded in by their seeming lack of space and by a rigid social order, Europeans looked with longing across the ocean where space and opportunity abounded. Time and again, men critical of their own society hoped by migration to find the scope for working out their visions of a better order.

Yet, in the actual coming, as likely as not, they encountered the standing quandary of the revolutionary. They had themselves been rebels in order to put into practice their ideas of a new society. But to do so they had to restrain the rebellion of others. As they laid out their communities they learned to fear the dangers that emanated from other dissenters unwilling to be bound by their restraints. The result was a long conflict between the demands of authority and the permissiveness of freedom. To a considerable measure, the American pattern of constitutional and responsible liberty emerged from more than three centuries of such conflict.

This process had already begun in the seventeenth century. The Puritan effort to create a Bible Commonwealth in New England was the product of the unsettlement of English society. For John Winthrop and his companions the New World was a New Canaan, set aside by Divine Providence as the field for their experiment. Yet once the Puritans had arrived, they encountered in disconcerting numbers a variety of visionaries whose individual conceptions of society threatened to destroy the whole community. It was manifestly dangerous to allow every man to build his own Utopia. The Puritans thus found it necessary, almost at once, to begin to delineate the lines between the freedom of the individual to follow his own dreams and the responsibility of the society for maintaining order.

The conflict was exposed in dramatic fashion in the career of the main mover of the Puritan migration and its most influential leader, John Winthrop. The vivid account of his life throws light on the whole movement from the start of the enterprise in England to the development of a flourishing society in Massachusetts Bay.

Oscar Handlin

Author's Preface

The Puritans of New England are not in good repute today. Authors and critics who aspire to any degree of sophistication take care to repudiate them. Liberals and conservatives alike find it advantageous to label the measures they oppose as Puritan. Whatever is wrong with the American mind is attributed to its Puritan ancestry, and anything that escapes these assaults is smothered under a homespun mantle of quaintness by lovers of the antique. Seventeenth-century Massachusetts has thus become in retrospect a preposterous land of witches and witch hunters, of killjoys in tall-crowned hats, whose main occupation was to prevent each other from having any fun and whose sole virtue lay in their furniture.

It is not likely that this vision will ever be wholly dispelled. We have to caricature the Puritans in order to feel comfortable in their presence. They found answers to some human problems that we would rather forget. Their very existence is therefore an affront, a challenge to our moral complacency; and the easiest way to meet the challenge is to distort it into absurdity, turn the challengers into fanatics. It is not hard to do, for there were real fanatics among them. Ironically, we have often given our praise to the fanatics, while the man who successfully fought them has received only the grudging admiration we accord to one who succeeds in a bad business.

Actually the central problem of Puritanism as it affected John Winthrop and New England has concerned men of principle in every age, not least of all our own. It was the question of what responsibility a righteous man owes to society. If society follows a course that he considers morally wrong, should he withdraw and keep his principles intact, or should he stay? Americans have answered the question in various ways. Henry Thoreau did not hesitate to reject a society that made war on Mexico. William Lloyd Garrison called on the North to leave the Union in order to escape complicity in the sin of slaveholding. John Winthrop had another answer, which colored his approach to every problem he confronted as a man and as governor of a Puritan colony. What his answer was this book attempts to show.

Edmund S. Morgan

Author's Preface to the Second Edition

In the forty years since this book was written, the inhabitants of seventeenth-century New England have undergone a closer scrutiny than any other set of people in American history. Scores of new studies have won them an intellectual respect they had only begun to enjoy in the 1930s. The Puritans themselves made the reassessment possible. They were so confident of the importance of what they were doing that they took time to record, explain, and justify it as they went along. The richness of the resulting record has enticed historians ever since but never more so than in recent years, perhaps because Americans have become less sure of what they are now doing and of who they are. In the effort to understand ourselves today, we can turn with fresh interest to a people who knew themselves and their mission in life so well.

After reconsidering the way I looked at the Puritans forty years ago, my own perspective remains much as it was. I retain an admiration for the courage of an Anne Hutchinson and a Roger Williams, but the dilemma that defined the life of John Winthrop still seems to me the key to understanding the Puritans and the enduring human problems that engaged them. Although I have learned from the new scholarship much that I did not know, and have altered a few passages accordingly, I think Winthrop speaks for the Puritans more convincingly now than ever. His dilemma, in one form or another, continues to trouble us as it troubled him. If we have anything to learn from the Puritans—and I believe we do—Winthrop remains our most challenging teacher. I hope this book conveys his message.

E. S. M.

The
Puritan Dilemma

I

The Taming of the Heart

When Henry VIII turned his back on the Pope, dissolved the monasteries, and confiscated their property, many Englishmen rejoiced. Their country could now join in the Protestant Reformation and gain a purer church. Adam Winthrop, a London cloth merchant with ready cash, was pleased for a simpler reason: he was able to buy part of the confiscated monastery at Bury St. Edmunds, in Suffolk. He paid the King £408, 11s. 3d. for the manor of Groton and thus transformed himself into a country gentleman. That was in 1544.

Forty-four years later, in the year when English sailors defeated the Spanish Armada, and with it the last serious effort by a Catholic power to recapture England for the Pope, John Winthrop was born, grandson to Adam. John's father, also called Adam, came into possession of Groton Manor a few years after John's birth and brought his family to live there on the old monastic estate.

Groton was a good place to grow up in—gently rolling country, checkered with dark wood lots and bright fields of wheat, rye, peas, barley, hops, with here and there a shallow pond, stocked with fat carp, which were harvested regularly like any other crop. The heart of the place was a huge half-timbered barn whose steep thatched roof covered the stalls of cart horses, milk cattle, and a few fine saddle horses for the lord of the manor and his lady. And there was a great house, where John, the only son of the family, knew he would one day sit in his father's place and preside over the modest entourage of servants and tenants who lived in this small world.

Though small, it was not an isolated world. A constant procession of uncles and aunts and cousins marched through it, bearing strange tales of strange places. One had gone to Spain with the Earl of Essex to attack the Catholic king, but had been himself converted to Catholicism by a Jesuit priest. Another shuttled back and forth between Groton and Ireland, setting the ladies' tongues wagging wherever he went, and finally getting himself excommunicated, apparently because he failed to obtain a proper divorce from one wife before marrying another. The Winthrop tribe was a large one, and sooner or later, good or bad, they all showed up at Groton.

John's father, the second Adam Winthrop of Groton, was one of the good ones. He had been trained in the law, but after coming into possession of the manor he devoted himself entirely to the difficult business of making it a success. For nearly half a century prices had been rising all over England and Europe, with disastrous results for gentlemen like himself, who lived on the rents received from tenants. Rents were often fixed by law, so that they could not be raised to match the rise in prices, nor could the tenants be evicted. Such was the case with some of the lands at Groton; on the rest the lord of the manor could grow crops for his own use or for sale. Adam saw where the main chance lay and made the most of the untenanted lands. Groton was near enough to London to profit by the rising metropolitan demand for foodstuffs; and by the time John was five years old, Adam was collecting £62 a year from the sale of crops, a little more than he obtained from all his rents. In addition to Groton Manor, he held land as a tenant on three or four manors nearby, and he was constantly buying more. Adam was a country gentleman, but he was also a good businessman, and the Winthrop family fortunes rose steadily under his guidance. It would be up to John to keep them rising. From Adam he learned how.

What else John learned from his father or his mother would be hard to say. The few surviving letters of his mother's suggest that she was a pious woman, and he may have received a religious bent from her. However, with a Roman Catholic and an excommunicated bigamist familiar and welcome guests at the manor, the Winthrops cannot have been a narrow-minded family.

When John was seven, Adam was paying John Chaplyn, vicar of a nearby church, for "scholinge." The boy was evidently being prepared for college. It had already become fashionable for gentlemen and even noblemen to send their sons to the universities, and Suffolk men went to Cambridge. Adam himself had gone there, in fact had married as his first wife the sister of John Still, then master of Trinity College. Probably through this connection he gained the office of auditor at Trinity and St. John's, and every year in late November or early December mounted his horse and rode away to Cambridge to audit the accounts and renew old friendships. In 1602 on one of his regular trips he got his son admitted, and the following March John, now fifteen, went off to college.

Here the great Thomas Nevile, master of Trinity, was pulling down old buildings and throwing up new ones to produce the magnificent court with its great fountain in the center. At the same time he was making the college foremost in the university for scholarship. The students responded to his efforts not merely in their studies, but in ways that students esteem more highly than scholarship: they had "provision of stones layd up; and also of some bucketts to be provided to fetch water from her conduyt, to poure downne upon St. John's men." They also had a reputation for demonstrating their prowess in another manner: "Oh the greivous sinnes of T Colledg," sighed one pious student a few years before Winthrop entered, for the boys "had a woman which was from chamber to chamber on the night tyme."

How all this struck John Winthrop is hard to say. He later remembered that his "lusts were so masterly as no good could fasten upon mee," but this was a conventional way for men of his time to speak of their youth. He was certainly homesick: "I fell into a lingring feaver, which took away the comfort of my life. For being there neglected, and despised, I went up and down mourning with myself." Since it was not customary for sons of gentlemen to stay at college long enough for a degree anyhow, John was back at Groton within two years, ready to do his part in advancing the family fortunes.

Opportunity came quickly. About the time of his return Mr. John Forth of Great Stambridge in the neighboring county of Essex paid a visit to Adam Winthrop, and the two of them talked about a possible match between John and Forth's daughter Mary. It was proper for parents to arrange these things. The children might be consulted, but marriages involved the transfer of large amounts of property belonging to the parents. When a boy and girl were married, the father of each of them was expected to endow the couple with capital in land, goods, or money, and every father wished to make a good bargain, to get as much as possible out of the other father. Adam's bargain with Forth evidently was a favorable one and included large quantities of land. When John returned from Cambridge, he and his father rode to Great Stambridge, and on March 28, 1605, the couple were contracted, a ceremony corresponding to our engagement. Within three weeks they were married, John having then attained the age of seventeen. Ten months later he was a father.

It was a solemn young man who brought his youth to a close by so early a marriage. Somewhere, at Groton or Cambridge or Great Stambridge—it is impossible to say where—John Winthrop had caught a fever more lingering than the one that took away his comforts in college. He had caught the fever of Puritanism.

Superficially Puritanism was only a belief that the Church of England should be purged of its hierarchy and of the traditions and ceremonies inherited from Rome. But those who had caught the fever knew that Puritanism demanded more of the individual than it did of the church. Once it took possession of a man, it was seldom shaken off and would shape—some people would say warp—his whole life. Puritanism was a power not to be denied. It did great things for England and for America, but only by creating in the men and women it affected a tension which was at best painful and at worst unbearable. Puritanism required that a man devote his life to seeking salvation but told him he was helpless to do anything but evil. Puritanism required that he rest his whole hope in Christ but taught him that Christ would utterly reject him unless before he was born God had foreordained his salvation. Puritanism required that man refrain from sin but told him he would sin anyhow. Puritanism required that he reform the world in the image of God's holy kingdom but taught him that the evil of the world was incurable and inevitable. Puritanism required that he work to the best of his ability at whatever task was set before him and partake of the good things that God had filled the world with, but told him he must enjoy his work and his pleasures only, as it were, absentmindedly, with his attention fixed on God.

These paradoxical, not to say contradictory, requirements affected different people in different ways. Some lived in an agony of uncertainty, wondering each day whether God had singled them out for eternal glory or eternal torment. Some enjoyed a holy certainty and went their indomitable ways with never a look backward. Some spent their lives demonstrating to themselves and everyone else how holy they were. All labored hard, and some by so doing amassed great wealth or won fame among their fellow men—but never dared enjoy it.

Puritanism meant many things. But to young John Winthrop it principally meant the problem of living in this world without taking his mind off God. It would have been easier to withdraw from the world, as the monks and hermits did, to devote oneself wholly to God, but that was not permitted. Puritans must live in the world, not leave it. For a time Winthrop thought he would study divinity and enter the ministry. In that profession he might at least have been freed from the distractions of ordinary business in order to concentrate his attention on God. But his friends dissuaded him, and anyway it was not so much his business as his pleasures that laid snares for him. He was a countryman of simple tastes who liked good food, good drink, and good company. He liked his wife. He liked to stroll by the river with a fowling piece and have a go at the birds. He liked to smoke a pipe. He liked to tinker with gadgets. He liked all the things that God had given him, and he knew it was right to like them, because they were God-given. But how was one to keep from liking them too much? How love the world with moderation and God without?

After his marriage he tried one way after another to keep his exuberant worldly spirit within bounds and gradually denied himself many of the things that he liked most. He resolved, as he noted in a sporadic record he kept of his religious experiences, to give up his tinkering "and to content my selfe with such things as were lefte by our forefathers." He resolved to give up shooting, after a prolonged and revealing argument with himself. For one thing, he said, it was against the law, and "thoughe the lawe cannot binde from the use of the creatures, yet it may limitt the manner of taking them." It took too much time. It was too strenuous ("it toyles a mans bodye overmuch"). It was dangerous. It was expensive (if you were caught, the fine was more than a man ought to pay for such a sport). Finally he came to the most telling point: "lastly for mine owne part I have ever binne crossed in usinge it, for when I have gone about it not without some woundes of conscience, and have taken much paynes and hazarded my healthe, I have gotten sometimes a verye little but most commonly nothinge at all towards my cost and laboure." In other words, he was a poor shot!

To Winthrop there was nothing incongruous or hypocritical about this reasoning. Shooting was not a legitimate recreation for a Puritan unless he got a satisfaction from it proportionate to the time and effort it cost. No Puritan objected to recreation as such; indeed it was necessary for a man to indulge in frivolous pleasures from time to time, in order that he might return to his work refreshed. But to serve the purpose, recreation had to be fun and not exhaust a man physically or bore him or frustrate him. It was no fun for Winthrop to return weary from a shoot with nothing in his bag to hand his wife for dinner.

Dinner itself was another problem. He found that he liked his food too well and after a heavy meal was more ready to continue with other pleasures of the flesh than to go back to the tedious business of casting accounts and collecting rents. Whenever he indulged himself excessively in this or any other way he regretted it afterwards and compensated by an overzealous abstemiousness, so that for a time his life vibrated dizzily between indulgence and restraint: "When I had some tyme abstained from suche worldly delights as my heart most desired, I grewe very melancholick and uncomfortable, for I had been more careful to refraine from an outward conversation in the world, than to keepe the love of the world out of my heart, or to uphold my conversation in heaven; which caused that my comfort in God failinge, and I not daringe to meddle with any earthly delights, I grewe into a great dullnesse and discontent: which beinge at last perceived, I examined my heart, and findinge it needfull to recreate my minde with some outward recreation, I yielded unto it, and by a moderate exercise herein was much refreshed." But here grew the mischief: "I perceivinge that God and mine owne conscience did alowe me so to doe in my need, I afterwards tooke occasion, from the benefite of Christian libertie, to pretend need of recreation when there was none, and so by degrees I ensnared my heart so farre in worldly delights, as I cooled the graces of the spirit by them."

And so the cycle would begin again. It was no good to put temptations away; that was to live out of the world. Once when he had gone to London on a business trip, which freed him to enjoy God undistracted by the cares and pleasures that surrounded him at home—London itself apparently held no temptations for him—he found that he felt only a spiritual deadness, "without any great sence either of guilt or peace." From this experience he drew the appropriate Puritan conclusion, "that he which would have suer peace and joye in Christianitye, must not ayme at a condition retyred from the world and free from temptations, but to knowe that the life which is most exercised with tryalls and temptations is the sweetest, and will prove the safeste. For such tryalls as fall within compasse of our callinges, it is better to arme and withstande them than to avoide and shunne them."

This was what he had been telling himself all along and continued to tell himself again and again: "O Lord, crucifie the world unto me, that though I cannot avoyd to live among the baites and snares of it, yet it may be so truely dead unto me and I unto it, as I may no otherwise love, use, or delight in any the most pleasant, profitable, etc, earthly comforts of this life, than I doe the ayre which I continually drawe in, or the earthe which I ever tread upon, or the skye which I ever behould."

As the years went by and he kept repeating these injunctions to himself, Winthrop gradually reduced the extent of his oscillation between abstinence and excess. It took time, time to cool the blood, time to grow in the spiritual strength that alone could hold him to a steady course of godliness in a world of temptations. But in the end, before he was forty, he was successful in containing the tension. How successful was evident in his married life.

Marriage he knew to be a good thing, but like everything else it had to be prevented from becoming too good. A man must love his wife, and she must love him. Love was a duty and hopefully a pleasure too, but it must be kept within bounds. It must never exceed or overpower or in any way diminish love for God. The possibility of rivalry between these two kinds of love was no mere figure of speech, for the Puritan's religion was no desiccated moralism. The Puritan loved his God with all the sensual abandon he denied himself in dealing with the world. John Winthrop, who was generally considered a grave and sober man by his contemporaries, found the most suitable images for his religion in the Song of Solomon, and in a letter to a friend might suddenly turn to address God in an embarrassingly sexual apostrophe: "Drawe us with the sweetnesse of thine odours, that we may runne after thee, allure us, and speak kindly to thy servantes, that thou maist possess us as thine owne, in the kindnesse of youth and the love of mariage ... let us heare that sweet voyce of thine, my love my dove, my undefiled: spread thy skirt over us and cover our deformitye, make us sicke with thy love: let us sleep in thine armes, and awake in thy kingdome."

Some religions, recognizing the difficulty of reconciling this kind of heavenly passion with the love of a wife or mistress, have advocated celibacy. For the Puritan no such solution was open. He must know and enjoy both kinds of love at once.

John Winthrop's first wife was an earthly woman who listened patiently to his religious counsels and behaved herself as befitted the wife of a gentleman, but never caught the fire of Puritanism that burned in her husband. She bore him six children in ten years and died in 1615. Within six months he consoled himself by marrying Thomasine Clopton, a godly young woman of an old and respected Suffolk family. On the first anniversary of their wedding she too died, and after waiting a little over a year, at the age of thirty John married again, this time Margaret Tyndal, the daughter of Sir John Tyndal of Much Maplestead in Essex. As usual, John seems to have received a substantial dowry, but from Margaret's later letters it is evident that he received much more than that.

Margaret was a very womanly woman, one of the most appealing in American history. "A very gracious woman," her husband once called her, and the adjective was as fitting in the modern sense as in the religious one that he intended. Her letters, written in a neat and labored script, are full of tenderness, as for example when her husband was in London and afflicted with a sore hand: "I will not looke for any longe letters this terme because I pitty your poore hande if I had it heare I would make more of it than ever I did, and bynde it up very softly for feare of hurting it." Or again, "It is now late and bed time and I must bid thee good night before I am wilinge for I could finde in my hart to sit and talke with thee all night." But she is as much a Puritan as her husband and never forgets that he is only a man and that her highest love must be reserved for God, who is pleased "to exercise us with one affliction after another in love, lest wee should forget our selves and love this world to much." She can even write, with no intention of irony, that a solemn letter of her husband's "did make a very good supply in stead of a sarmon."

John's letters during his occasional absences from Groton often had a good deal of the sermon about them, but they were never lacking in homely warmth. "It is now bedd tyme," he closes one, "but I must lye alone, therefore I make lesse haste." Every letter takes up the theme of their love and how it must lose itself in a higher love, but the tension has been contained, and he can slip easily from reflections on eternity to "I feared thou shouldst take could and therefore I have sent thee another garment." In Margaret Tyndal he had found a woman he could love without losing himself in mere earthly passion.

At thirty Winthrop had become familiar with himself. He knew what temptations were likely to conquer him, and he had discovered how to meet them. Above all else he had learned to stick to business. If he worked hard at whatever task lay before him, he could take his pleasures in stride. Of course work itself could be a snare. It was easy to become engrossed in it for its own sake or for the sake of the worldly rewards it brought. A man who labored merely for gain, with no thought for God, was no better than a libertine. But he who worked because God willed it, multiplying his talents like a good and faithful servant, could throw himself into his job almost as a way of worship, without fear of losing balance. That he might amass a fortune in the process was an incidental benefit, not to be treated as a goal, but not to be rejected if it came. Though Winthrop was a notably conscientious worker, he apparently had no difficulty in maintaining the right attitude to his work. It never obscured his view of God as the pleasures of the flesh so often did.

Winthrop's principal work during the early years of his first marriage was doubtless the management of his estate. For three years he and his bride lived on at Groton, where, under Adam's watchful eye, he could collect rents and fines from tenants and supervise the farming without exposing his estate to the dangers of youth and inexperience. From Groton the couple moved to Mary's home in Great Stambridge, where the dowry lands were located. In both places, along with advice in managing his own lands, he probably received the opportunity to participate in running the larger parental estates.

During these same years he began the study of law. Perhaps the ordinary affairs of a country gentleman left him with more free time than a conscientious Puritan gentleman could legitimately claim for recreation; or perhaps he made time for study, because a knowledge of the law would better enable him to perform the work in life which God had set him. As future lord of Groton Manor he would need to know something of the law or else hire someone who did, for at regular intervals, probably every three weeks, he would have to hold a manorial court at which his tenants might sue each other in a wide variety of small actions. The lord of the manor did not have to preside himself. Adam Winthrop occasionally held courts for neighboring lords, and when John was twenty-one, on a visit home from Stambridge, Adam let him hold his first court at Groton, presumably to give him a little experience in a job that would occupy him extensively in the future.

Holding manorial court was good training not only for a future lord of the manor, but for any gentleman who might someday wish to practice law. That John Winthrop may have been thinking of this possibility is suggested by the fact that in 1613 he was admitted to Gray's Inn, one of the Inns of Court in London, where young gentlemen studied law. How long he stayed there is not evident, but by 1617 he was back in Suffolk as one of the county's justices of the peace, a post reserved for persons of importance—and importance meant property.

By the criterion of property John Winthrop was becoming a man of importance. Sometime before 1618 his father turned over the lordship of Groton Manor to him. This,

combined with the properties acquired through his different wives, must have left him better off than his father had
been. Adam, at any rate, seems never to have held the office of justice. Though John did not hold it continuously, it
gave him a larger acquaintance with the law than he could
have gained in the manorial court, for the quarter sessions
of the justices of the peace tried almost every kind of crim-
inal case except those involving treason. Moreover, as a
justice, John gained something that might prove more
valuable to his career than a knowledge of the law—a familiarity with the other big men of the county.

From his point of view this was not all gain. Though he
kept himself strictly to business, working at his job with
the devotion that he knew God demanded of him, he
found that the other justices took a somewhat lighter view
of their duties and of the world in general. For a man who
was doing his best to keep his earthly passions in check, it
was a trying experience to come up against some of these
confident squires. "Methought," he wrote later, "I hearde
all men tellinge me I was a foole, to sett so light by honour, credite, welthe, jollitie etc: which I sawe so many wise
men so much affecte and joye in, and to tye my comforte
to a conversation in heaven, which was no where to be
seene, no way regarded, which would bring my selfe and
all my gifts into contempt." He comforted himself with
the fact that the servants of God always meet with contempt in this world, and fortified himself as he trotted to
or from the sessions by saying prayers and singing psalms.

In spite of his meticulous attention to duty, in spite of
his want of humor and his psalm-singing, it is unlikely
that many of his new associates laughed at him. He was
not the only Puritan gentleman in Suffolk. Sir Nathaniel
Barnardiston, as big a man as you could find outside the
ranks of the nobility, with an estate said to be worth
£4000 a year, was a Puritan too. His grandfather had been
educated under Calvin at Geneva, during the exile of the

Protestants in the days of Queen Mary, and he himself was as ardent a believer as Winthrop. Moving into the circle occupied by the leading men of the country, Winthrop found others who shared his views, men with their eyes on heaven but their hands in the everyday business of their callings. Through these men of consequence Winthrop felt his own world expand. His father had once studied law in London, but had then retired to the fastness of Groton Manor. For Adam, Groton was world enough. John was moving along another path, toward a larger world.

As he moved, the problem of living in the world assumed new dimensions. He had learned to discipline himself, to use the good things of the earth without being used by them. But as he moved out from Groton Manor into a position of prominence in the county, as he joined in executing the laws of the land, he could not fail to see that living in the world demanded more than a taming of the heart. The world itself required discipline. Though a Puritan must live in it, he need not, must not, take it as he found it. The world, within limits, was plastic, and Winthrop was beginning to feel that he should lend a hand in shaping it.

II

Evil and Declining Times

From the day man first thought of God, the world has never seemed pure enough. Puritans knew it never could be, but they felt a compelling obligation to do battle with its impurities. The obligation, as they saw it, had always existed, although the Roman Catholic Church had closed men's eyes to it until the Reformation. God, it was clear to the Puritans, demanded perfect obedience, and men must never cease trying to give it.

They knew the attempt could not succeed, for men were moral cripples, incapacitated forever by Adam's fall. They might be kept from murder but not from hate, from adultery but not from lust, from theft but not from greed. However good their intentions, however unrelenting their efforts, the evil in their hearts would always betray them and bar the doors of heaven. But if the assault on wickedness would help no man toward salvation—only Christ could do that—it would not be without results in this world. God recognized degrees of evil and rewarded men's minor victories over it with minor rewards. He brought prosperity and health to nations which prevented or punished murder, adultery, theft, and other open breaches of His commands.

Every nation or people, the Puritans believed, existed by virtue of a covenant with God, an agreement whereby they promised to abide by His laws, and He in turn agreed to treat them well. To help carry out their part of the bargain, people instituted governments, and the business of government was to enforce God's laws by punishing every detectable breach. Government in this view had a sacred task and enjoyed divine sanction in carrying it out. The institution of government, however, did not absolve the people from responsibility. As long as the government did its job, the people must give it all the assistance in their power. But if the governors failed in their sacred task and fell prey to the evils they were supposed to suppress, then the people must rebel and replace the wicked rulers with better ones. If they did not, God would descend in fire and brimstone to punish the whole nation.

Unfortunately, in this world of imperfections one could not always say with confidence whether or not the government was doing its job adequately. In England the Puritans in the sixteenth and early seventeenth centuries generally thought it was not, but, except during a few unhappy years under Mary Tudor, they did not find its failures bad enough to warrant rebellion. When Mary Tudor tried to return England to the Pope, they had no hesitation in calling for her head. They did not get it, and she got many of theirs, but they did enjoy a rare certitude.

After Mary died, her sister Elizabeth kept the Puritans guessing. Her government did not satisfy them, for she did not purify the church of its ceremonies and vestments. She did not do away with bishops and archbishops. She did not enforce a proper observance of the Sabbath. But she did defy the Pope. She did make England a bulwark of Protestantism against the Catholic power of Spain. She even accepted a few Puritans among her advisers. And she did make every Englishman think it a privilege to be ruled by her. In the sixteenth century, as in the eighteenth, men were disposed to suffer while evils were sufferable, and Elizabeth seemed eminently sufferable. Puritans complained and protested, but they told themselves that things were moving their way.

Under Elizabeth's successor, James I, it was less easy but not impossible to keep up this belief. James made no secret of his dislike for Puritans and promised to harry them out of the land. But his bark proved worse than his bite. He appointed as Archbishop of Canterbury George Abbot, an easygoing prelate who leaned toward Puritanism himself. And while James allowed no further reformation of the church, he did pick a fight with the Roman Catholics over the power of a king to defend the laws of God inside his kingdom without interference from the Pope. Though the Puritans thought that James was doing a poor job of defending those laws, they had to applaud his attack on the Pope.

And so they were drawn into uneasy complicity in a regime they considered no more than half right. In addition to the burden of guilt each of them carried for his own sins, they became increasingly troubled by the sins of the nation. Whenever drought, disease, or depression appeared, they looked fearfully for worse to come, because they knew that worse was deserved, that God would not always tolerate the evils that the English Government tolerated, nay practiced. Preachers sounded the alarm again and again, calling up the memory of Sodom and Gomorrah: "Though England be a Paradise for pleasure, a storehouse of wealth, and a rich Exchequer of all plenty and delights; and though London be the Kings Chamber, the seat of the Nobles, the Mart of rich and worthy Marchants, and indeede the beauty of the whole land, yet if God once visit this land and citie, for the sinnes of the inhabitants thereof, neither this nor that, neither the largeness of their territories, nor their beauty, excellence, riches, or multitude of people shall excuse them, but he will make them as Sodom, and like unto Gomorrha."

This was the England that Winthrop knew, an England full of plenty and delights but under the shadow of God's wrath. As he grew older the shadow deepened. In the

1620's the textile industry suffered a depression that affected the whole country. Clothworkers were unemployed, hungry but unable to pay for country produce; clothiers could not market their fabrics; farmers could not pay their rents. The cost of caring for the poor and unemployed rose steadily. Was this not a hint of God's displeasure, a warning of worse to come?

Winthrop's own county of Suffolk, a textile center, was especially hard hit by the depression, and it became increasingly difficult for Winthrop to support his family on the proceeds of his lands. In the 1620's he was still a young man, in his thirties, but his children were growing up and would soon have to be launched in the world. The eldest, John, Jr., would come of age in 1627. Besides John there were Henry, Forth, and Mary, the other surviving children of his first wife. Margaret had borne him three sons, Stephen, Adam, and Deane, and there would be more coming. For a time he thought of moving the whole family to Ireland and striking out afresh, as one of his uncles had done. Instead he went more and more often to London, to expand his shrinking resources through the legal business available there. For a while he seems to have served as counsel to a Parliamentary committee engaged in drafting legislation, and in 1627 he found what many a gentleman in his predicament before and since have looked for, a job with the government. He was appointed common attorney in His Majesty's Court of Wards and Liveries.

The Court of Wards was an archaic institution, devised to administer the lands of the King's wards. These wards were minors who fell heir to land held directly from the King, land, for instance, like Groton Manor. If Winthrop died before his eldest son came of age, the boy would become the King's ward, subject to his direction in all things, including marriage; and for the duration of the boy's minority the King would be entitled to the use of all the

Winthrop lands, even those not held directly from the Crown. The court no longer attempted to manage the lands or to bring up the King's wards. Instead, it sold his rights over a particular ward to the highest bidder. It was, in fact, a royal real estate and revenue bureau with power not only to sell wardships but also to sit as a court in disputes arising about them. Anyone engaged in such a dispute had to employ one of the common attorneys, and as there were only two besides Winthrop, a great deal of business, for which he could charge a respectable fee, would automatically fall in his lap.

Winthrop was lucky to get the job, but it was not without drawbacks. It meant that he would have to be away from home and Margaret more than ever. The court sat four times a year in sessions that lasted from three to seven weeks, and during all these times he would have to be in London, where life was close and cramped for a man used to the broad fields of Suffolk. Winthrop escaped much of the loneliness that a countryman usually finds in the city, for he had a growing number of relatives there. His younger sister Lucy, still in her twenties, was Mrs. Emmanuel Downing. Her husband was one of the other common attorneys in the Court of Wards and probably helped get the job for Winthrop. An older sister, Anne, had married Thomas Fones, a London apothecary. Though Anne had died several years before and Fones had remarried, Winthrop still called him brother, and his new wife was "Sister Fones," for a relationship once established was seldom broken. (When Fones himself died, Winthrop helped Sister Fones choose another husband, Henry Paynter, and thereafter he always referred to them as Brother and Sister Paynter!) With every new brother and sister Winthrop acquired an additional flock of relatives, all ready to welcome him to their own family circles. He had generally stayed with the Downings or the Foneses on his previous trips to London, but now that he was to be in the city regularly he set up bachelor's quarters among the other lawyers in the Inner Temple.

There, of an evening, before slipping into a cold bed, he would light a candle and write a few words to Margaret. Pen and ink were a sorry substitute for her presence, but at least he could have the feeling, however remote, that he was talking with her, answering her questions about Brother and Sister Downing and Brother and Sister Fones ("we have received all the thinges you sent, my sister and my self thanke thee for them"), pouring out his own warm feeling for her, but always careful to guide it toward the thought of heaven, which could sustain him in a cold London lodging as well as at Groton Manor—"so I kisse my sweet wife and rest thy faithfull husband."

After putting up with this kind of life for a while they both thought of moving the family to London, where they could be together. Winthrop looked for a house, but like other countrymen moving to the city he had difficulty finding one large enough to suit him at a price he could pay. He thought of settling in Rotherhithe, a suburb about nine miles down the river, but Margaret vetoed the idea: she was afraid that the daily commuting to London (by water) would be dangerous, especially in winter. "I did confir with my mother about it," she wrote, meaning *his* mother, "and she thinkes you had better take a house in the city, and so come home to your own table and familye and I am of the same minde but I shall alwayes submit to what you shal thinke fit." So nothing came of that idea.

The work of an attorney in the Court of Wards was, on the whole, dull; much of the time Winthrop found himself functioning as a high-class errand boy. The court itself, where the actions were tried, adjoined Westminster Hall, but many of the officers whom an attorney had to consult did business in quarters scattered all over the city. Winthrop tramped through the streets from one office to another, a man with full, Elizabethan beard, large eyes, long nose, pushing through crowds, hastening past open sewers and occasional evil-smelling heaps of ordure, stumbling through dark lanes where the overhanging houses nearly met overhead, and taking passage for Westminster by way of the river in order to attend at court. There he would argue the case of a client—perhaps a widow bidding for the wardship of her young son's lands, or trying to prove that the Crown had no right to them. When the court adjourned, he would be off again on other business.

In spite of its drawbacks, the job did offer Winthrop some opportunities. He met and exchanged information with consequential people from all over England, brushed elbows with members of Parliament, and lived at the center of England, where he could watch the country being ruled. And as he became familiar with London, that beauty of the land, that chamber of the King and seat of the nobles, he could not fail to sniff the evil at the core of the English Government. Indeed, his own job was a rotten one, for the very existence of the Court of Wards was an insult to justice. Wardship had originated when the King needed to guarantee that each of his tenants would be a fighting man ready to support him on the field of battle. Now it was simply a way to make money out of the misfortunes of widows and orphans. The King used it for all it was worth, and so did the buyers of wardships. When a ward came of age, his lands were returned to him with wood lots leveled, fields depleted, and buildings deteriorated, sometimes to the point of ruin.

The way the court was run offered eloquent testimony to the government's corruption. The Master of the Wards (head of the court) was expected as a matter of course to derive a handsome private income from selling wardships to friends and favorites. Winthrop's job presented no such temptations, and he himself never commented on the corruption of the court in any of his surviving papers, but he must have known, as his friend Hugh Audley, the cynical auditor of the court, once remarked, that the master's office "might be worth some thousands of pounds to him who would go, after his death, instantly to heaven; twice as much to him who would go to purgatory; and nobody knows what to him who would adventure to go to hell."

Winthrop seems to have regarded Sir Robert Naunton, the master during his own attorneyship, as one who aimed at heaven, but there was no blinking the foulness of the whole administration of wardships, or, for that matter, of the whole process of government. And a government so corrupt could not be much concerned about the virtue of its citizens, about the nation's covenant with God. The eyes of good Puritans were continually affronted by open breaches of God's commands. Wickedness lay everywhere unrebuked.

In this situation the Puritans did what they could to save the country from impending doom. Their preachers called ever more loudly for reform, and laymen, where they had the opportunity, did more than talk. Justices of the peace like Winthrop exerted themselves to punish sin through the available laws. In Parliament, where Puritans were generally a vociferous minority if not a majority, they tried to make the right laws available. Winthrop never entered Parliament himself, but he did busy himself to get the right men elected from Suffolk, and among his papers is the draft of a bill against drunkenness, a subject which the House of Commons discussed at some length in the 1620's.

Parliament was, in fact, the bright hope of Puritans in their efforts to avert God's wrath. Under Elizabeth and James it had felt its way toward a share in the sovereign power and was responsible for whatever progress England had made in enforcing God's laws. In the summer of 1625, when London was frightened by the plague, the Reverend John Preston, one of the Puritans' most illustrious preachers, spoke before the House of Commons and reminded the members "that the Lord regards not so much what the particular sins of a Nation or Church are, as what the Action, the behaviour, the carriage of the State towards them is. Doubtlesse the action of both the Houses of Parliament declaring their zeale both now and heretofore, hath beene a great meanes of turning away the Lords wrath, and will be more and more, if you doe so more and more."

Unfortunately, even while Preston spoke, this great means of turning the Lord's wrath away from England faced the threat of extinction. Charles I, who replaced his father, James I, early in 1625, at once demonstrated a frightening lack of respect for the newly won authority of Parliament. When his first Parliament refused to grant him the funds he wanted and began to talk about his policies, he dissolved it. When he summoned a new Parliament, he had Bishop Laud preach to the members on the duty of obedience and warned them himself "that Parliaments are altogether in my power for their calling, sitting, and dissolution; therefore, as I find the fruits of them good or evil, they are to continue, or not to be." When this Parliament, too, began talking about matters which he did not think concerned the members, he sent them home and proceeded to the task of raising money by a forced loan, demanding it of taxpayers as though the Parliament had levied it as a tax. The forced loan precipitated a spirited resistance in which several Puritan gentlemen took part. Winthrop was probably not among them, for he does not seem to have got into trouble over it, as his friend Sir Nathaniel Barnardiston did. Barnardiston went to prison for refusing to pay, and so did another friend of Winthrop's, Sir Francis Barrington. Winthrop sent his son, John, Jr., to visit Barrington in prison ("but you must doe it in private") and tell him how things were going in Suffolk.

With the accession of Charles, the Puritans were dismayed by the turn for the worse not only in government but also in religion. Charles was married to a Catholic princess and was rightly suspected of being soft about Catholicism. He did not embrace it himself, but he did promote a religious doctrine almost equally bad in the eyes of Puritans. The Anglican Church, as established by Elizabeth, had espoused a moderate Calvinist theology which the Puritans could interpret as consonant with their own; but during the reign of James many of the church's leaders had fallen into the heresy known to Puritans as Arminianism, a belief that men by their own will power could achieve faith and thus win salvation. The Puritans had already become alarmed by the growth of this heresy and by the zeal of its advocates, when Charles ascended the throne and made plain his own fondness for it. The Arminians, and especially William Laud, whom Charles made Bishop of London in 1628, returned the favor by using their pulpits to preach the authority of kings and to support the forced loan. Old Archbishop Abbot, who for so many years had made life bearable for the Puritans, daringly opposed the loan and as a penalty found his authority in church courts transferred to a commission with Laud at its head. The King ruled the Anglican Church. Consistently, as places in it fell vacant, Arminians were promoted to fill them. "What do the Arminians hold?" it was asked, and Puritans gave the bitter answer: "All the best livings in England."

As the evils in church and state multiplied, Puritans looked more and more to Parliament for relief. With incredible boldness one of their preachers published *An Appeal to the Parliament,* calling upon the members not to allow themselves to be dissolved again until they had purged the country of all bishops. "Your Honours know," he told them, "that everie dissolution of a Parliament, without reall reformation, is against *right, reason,* and *record.* Is it not the right of the State, to be disburdened of caterpillars, moathes, and Canker-wormes; and of such *Lions* and *Beares,* as devour *Religion,* and *State-Policie?*

... Then stand your ground, and *quite your selves like men* in this matter of reformation." Egged on by pleas like this, the Commons grew more assertive. They demanded an end to unparliamentary taxation and the suppression of Arminianism in the church. They even passed a resolution that anyone who attempted to bring in either popery or Arminianism should be accounted a capital enemy of the King and kingdom. The implication was not lost on Charles: by this test he would be his own worst enemy. A week later, on March 10, 1629, he formally dissolved Parliament and made it plain that he did not intend to call another.

Thus the last bulwark against heresy and sin crumbled. Without Parliament there was scarcely a hope left of enforcing the will of God in England. On the Continent, too, Protestantism was sinking. Richelieu had taken La Rochelle, and the French Huguenots, who had risen in rebellion against a Catholic king, were in desperate straits. In Germany, Wallenstein was pulverizing the armies of the Protestants, and the Roman Church had recovered vast properties. It looked as though God had given over all Europe to the forces of evil, preparatory to wholesale destruction. In London, attending his dreary business at the Court of Wards, Winthrop sat down with a heavy heart to write to Margaret. "It is a great favour," he told her, "that we may enjoye so much comfort and peace in these so evill and declininge tymes and when the increasinge of our sinnes gives us so great cause to looke for some heavy Scourge and Judgment to be comminge upon us: the Lorde hath admonished, threatened, corrected, and astonished us, yet we growe worse and worse, so as his spirit will not allwayes strive with us, he must needs give waye to his furye at last; he hath smitten all the other Churches [in Europe] before our eyes, and hath made them to drinke of the bitter cuppe of tribulation, even unto death; we sawe this, and humbled not ourselves, to turne from our evill wayes, but have provoked him more than all the nations rounde about us: therefore he is turninge the cuppe towards us also, and because we are the last, our portion must be, to drinke the very dreggs which remaine: my dear wife, I am veryly perswaded, God will bringe some heavye Affliction upon this lande, and that speedylye."

Responsibility for England's wickedness lay heavy on Winthrop's shoulders. He had shared in the government of his county as justice of the peace, of his country as attorney in the Court of Wards. The utmost he and his Puritan friends could do in their various offices was not enough to stem the tide of evil. If God should descend in His wrath to punish England, as she so justly deserved, John Winthrop knew he would suffer with the rest. Not even if he resigned his offices and led the holiest of lives as a private citizen could he escape responsibility, for where governors failed to uphold God's laws, God held the governed accountable. Was there, then, no escape?

One way was revolution. If a ruler violated his trust, as Charles was doing, he might be deposed and replaced by one who would fulfill the people's covenant with God. But it was not easy for an Englishman to think of laying hands on his King, and besides there was the example of the Huguenots, who had tried and failed. Ultimately England would come to revolution, but not until the situation became more obviously desperate.

There was still another way out, but almost equally fearful. This was in effect to launch a second Protestant Reformation, to give up England and the Church of England as beyond saving and to withdraw from them as they had withdrawn from Rome a hundred years before. To many this was a tempting solution. To Winthrop and his family it would have furnished an escape from the contagious wickedness that surrounded them and, through repudiation, a freedom from responsibility. But Winthrop and most other Puritans rejected this solution.

Those who did take it were called Separatists. They would have nothing to do with the Anglican Church at all—and some went so far as to cut themselves off even more completely by immigration to Holland and then to Plymouth Plantation in New England. Every age has its own separatists. They are the intransigents, the undeviating purists who have to be right whatever the cost, who would sacrifice the world rather than compromise their own righteousness. But most Puritans saw that the problem of sin could not be escaped so easily, and most were sufficiently charitable toward their neighbors to think that England and her churches were still worth saving. The churches were corrupt, yes, but not so corrupt as to lose the name of church. They should be purified of their unregenerate members, their heretical clergymen, their unwarranted ceremonies, their bishops and archbishops, but they were nevertheless churches and must be embraced as churches. They had brought the means of salvation to many of their members and might still do so. To deny them would be to deny Christ and to arrogate a righteousness that belonged only to Him.

This was part of the same large paradox that had troubled Winthrop from the beginning, the paradox that required a man to live in the world without being of it. The obligation was not simply a trial imposed on saints in order to test their strength. It was a recognition that all men were brothers in sin, that there was no escape in this life from the evils that the monks in one way and the separatists in another were trying to put behind them. Though the Puritan must constantly bear witness against sin, though he must cause it to be punished by hanging and branding and cropping of ears, he must do so with the full knowledge that he too was guilty in heart if not in deed. Though he must do what he could to prevent and punish evil, yet if he failed, he could not wash his hands of the world and resign it to the forces of darkness. The separatists in their simplicity, their forthrightness, and their courage defied a wicked world. But their defiance was also a desertion. They failed their fellow men. They abandoned a charity to which the Puritans held fast. The men and women who hated evil as much as the separatists did but refused to turn their backs on their brethren were following the path that Puritanism (indeed, Christianity), in its deepest meaning, commanded.

In 1629 it was an increasingly dangerous and difficult path, while the way of separation looked more and more enticing. The more wicked the Anglican churches became, the harder it was for Puritans to treat them as true churches. Surely God's patience would be exhausted sooner or later. If, as all Protestants maintained, the Roman Church was incurable in the sixteenth century, perhaps the Anglican Church would prove so in the seventeenth. There would be no virtue in cleaving to it any longer than God did, yet to desert sooner would be equally wrong.

In this predicament, the course that finally appeared to Winthrop and a number of his friends was one that enabled them to avoid the problem rather than solve it: to leave England altogether, yet leave it with the approbation of the King and without repudiating its churches and the Christians in them.

III

A Shelter and a
Hiding Place

The idea of going to the New World was not novel. For more than a century Englishmen and other Old World travelers had drifted back and forth across the Atlantic, coasting the shores of North America, looking for a way through to the Pacific, looking for gold, catching fish, and trading with the strange people they encountered. The people had little to trade except for the furs of American animals, but what they got in return was more than the cloth and kettles and trinkets offered to them. The Europeans unwittingly brought with them a host of diseases— tuberculosis, diphtheria, smallpox—against which the native inhabitants had none of the biological immunities that the winnowing of centuries had conferred on the population of the Old World. As a result, by the time Winthrop and his friends thought of settling across the seas, massive epidemics had wiped out most of the men and women who might have stood in their way. By 1629 a few English settlers and fishermen had already moved in, planting themselves here and there along the American coast and on the islands that stood off it, learning to live from the land, with the assistance of the surviving natives (who nevertheless continued to die both silently and violently from the contact).

The King of England had no hesitation in laying claim to the whole continent, or of authorizing his subjects to people it for him. They had settled Virginia in 1607; and although the colonists had perished at first almost as rapidly as they came, two or three thousand of them were well established now. Others had colonized Bermuda and Barbados. In New England a group of Separatists had been living at Plymouth since 1620; and in 1623 a contingent of fishermen and farmers put down at Cape Ann, backed by a company of merchants calling themselves the Dorchester Adventurers. Though the merchants gave up by 1627 and most of the settlers returned to England, a few hung on in a village they named Salem.

In the circles where Winthrop moved, among the Puritan gentry of the eastern counties, there had been interest in colonization even before Charles I's final dissolution of Parliament in 1629. Noblemen with Puritan leanings had already invested in such ventures and showed a continuing interest that can scarcely be attributed to any financial returns they obtained. The founding of colonies was a notoriously unprofitable activity, and though the hope of striking it rich still led otherwise sane businessmen to invest modestly in colonies, there was probably a thought in the minds of many Puritans who squandered their money this way that a colony in the New World, if managed properly, might prove a port in the storm that was obviously brewing. Some wanted to acquire an island in the West Indies; others favored New England.

Actually a group of gentlemen and noblemen known as the Council for New England had already received a royal grant to the whole of New England in 1620. They had not yet made a serious colonizing effort, but they were willing to allow settlements on their land; and in 1628 they granted a charter to a group of Puritan merchants organized as the New England Company. The charter authorized the company to settle and govern the area from three miles south of the Charles River to three miles north of the Merrimack. This tract included the settlement at Salem, and the company immediately sent over Captain John Endecott, a veteran of the Dutch wars and a good Puritan, to take charge there. With him they sent a shipload of servants whom he was to employ in collecting the commodities supposed to abound in the country—sarsaparilla and sassafras (valued at the time as medicines), furs, and silk grass.

John Winthrop was not a member of the New England Company, and he was not optimistic about the prospects of colonial life. His second son, Henry, had gone to Barbados to make his fortune in 1627 and returned two years later with expensive habits and no fortune. But Barbados was not a Puritan settlement. When his oldest son, John, Jr., proposed to join Endecott's group, Winthrop received the idea favorably, if not enthusiastically. "I know not wheare you should goe with such religious company and under such hope of blessinge," he told his son, but urged him not to commit himself permanently to living in the New World. John thought it over, decided to try the Mediterranean instead, and went off on a fourteen-month tour of Constantinople, Leghorn, and Venice. Before he returned, the New England Company had been transformed into the Massachusetts Bay Company, and John Winthrop himself was deeply interested in it. There had evidently been some doubt about the validity of the charter from the Council for New England, and before investing heavily in the region, the members of the New England Company wished to make their title to it more secure. In March 1629, just a week before Charles dissolved his last Parliament, they managed—how is not clear—to obtain a royal charter confirming the grant and changing the name of the company to the Governor and Company of the Massachusetts Bay in New England.

Winthrop was at Groton when the royal charter was

granted but took the road shortly afterwards to attend the Easter term of court. At London he found gentlemen putting their heads together over a bottle to whisper things that one no longer dared to speak aloud. Parliament was at an end; Arminian prelates were riding high; the Tower was loaded with Puritan patriots. Everywhere, for those who could see through the glitter of Charles's self-assurance, the clouds of God's wrath seemed to be gathering. Members of the Massachusetts Bay Company were looking toward their colony with quickened interest. Winthrop doubtless talked with some of them. Possibly he already had emigration in mind when he wrote home to Margaret on May 15, 1629, "If the Lord seeth it wilbe good for us, he will provide a shelter and a hidinge place for us and ours."

A fortnight later he was able to snatch a brief holiday at Groton before the Trinity term of court began on June 5. As he and Margaret sat together in the long June evenings there was much to talk about: not only the alarming degeneration of the country but the even more spectacular degeneration of their son Henry, who had been painting the town red ever since his return from Barbados. On a visit to Uncle Fones in London he had turned the household into a veritable inn for his riotous companions and on top of that had wooed and won his cousin Bess, Fones's daughter, without so much as a by-your-leave from her father. Fones told Winthrop, "They both pretend to have proceeded so far that there is no recalling of it." They had been hastily married and shipped off to Groton for a honeymoon. But both John and Margaret feared that Henry had not yet settled down, and it would be easy for a father to think that the boy might behave in a more godly fashion if he lived in a more godly community. At any rate, Winthrop thought more and more of New England, and Margaret, being the woman she was, doubtless assured him that she would follow wherever he led.

Winthrop returned to his duties in London to find that his brother-in-law, Emmanuel Downing, was leaning strongly in the same direction, and he wrote at once to Margaret, "I am still more confirmed in that course which I propounded to thee." Two weeks later he sent her news "that wilbe more wellcome to thee, than a greate deale of other. My Office is gone, and my chamber, and I shalbe a saver in them both: so as I hope, we shall now enjoye each other againe as we desire." Possibly Winthrop resigned the office voluntarily in preparation for emigration. But whether he left England or not, his work in London was hardly worth continuing. The expense of travel and lodgings ate up most of the extra earnings, and since the doors to preferment were now closing against Puritans, the job was unlikely to be a springboard to a higher and more effective public office, which might have compensated for the pain of being so often separated from Margaret.

Though he had not yet made a firm decision to leave England, he had certainly begun to lean in that direction. As he himself later phrased it, "when God intendes a man to a worke he setts a Byas on his heart so as tho' he be tumbled this way and that yet his Bias still drawes him to that side, and there he restes at last." Winthrop's bias was now drawing him toward New England. To be sure that God had set it in him, he analyzed the problem of emigration as though it were a legal case, himself the client, and amassed evidence from as many sources as he could reach: from the directors of the Massachusetts Bay Company to satisfy himself of their motives and of the likelihood of success; from the Puritan clergymen he knew, for their opinion of its acceptability to God; from his friends, because they knew him and his situation and would not hesitate to speak plainly if they detected self-deception in his decisions. The sum of all the evidence he incorporated into a remarkable series of documents, designed to convince himself and others of the desirability of moving to

New England. They were circulated among important Puritans and were a powerful persuasive to Winthrop's contemporaries.

Winthrop had no desire to become a martyr. His arguments were those of a man accustomed to success and intending to have more of it. Several arguments demonstrated that England offered fewer opportunities for worldly success than America. "This land growes wearye of her Inhabitants," he wrote, referring to the depression which had put so many people, especially in Suffolk, out of work. People were too extravagant: a man was hard pressed to "keep sayle with his equalls," and all arts and trades were "carried in that deceiptfull and unrighteous course, as it is allmost impossible for a good and upright man to maintaine his charge and live comfortably in any of them," even an attorney in the Court of Wards. Indeed, in no trade could one expect a suitable recompense for time and labor, "except falshood he admitted to equall the balance." At the same time land was so hard to come by that men would spend as much for an acre or two as would buy many hundreds in America.

But wait. The King might lay claim to the continent, but what about the people already living there? Winthrop had heard of the epidemics that had wiped out so many, though he could scarcely have known how many, and he saw in their destruction the hand of God making way for the godly. Those who remained alive would have no need for the vast tracts of land around them. There would be, he argued, "more than enough for them and us," especially as he had heard that "they inclose no ground, neither have they cattell to maintayne it." So "why may not christians have liberty to go and dwell amongst them in their waste lands and woods (leaving them such places as they have manured for their corne) as lawfully as Abraham did among the Sodomites?" The translation of Indians into Sodomites was more than a figure of speech, for

Europeans had already formed an enduring image of native Americans as savages under the thrall of Satan. Christians moving in among them would help save their souls and improve their lives, even while the Christians made the most of their own God-given talents in exploiting the opportunities of the New World.

Those opportunities probably figured more largely in Winthrop's religious consciousness than any missionary impulse. Just as he considered hunting with a gun a bad form of recreation because he got so little profit from it, so the move to New England would be wrong unless there was a good chance that the colony could be an economic success. A man's duty to God was to work at his calling and improve his talents like a good and faithful servant. If he could do it better in New England than in old, that was good reason for moving. God was the overwhelming reality, indeed the only reality. Success and failure were relevant only as indications, and not always reliable ones, of His satisfaction or displeasure with a man's efforts to serve Him as he passed through life.

In framing his arguments Winthrop relied heavily on the opinions and advice of the Puritan ministers he most respected. The most compelling argument on his list was the judgment which they thought God would shortly bring upon England. "All other Churches of Europe are brought to desolation," he wrote, "and it cannot be, but the like Judgment is comminge upon us: And who knows, but that God hath provided this place, to be a refuge for manye, whom he meanes to save out of the general destruction." He recorded the objection raised by some of his friends, that "we have feared a Judgment a longe tyme, but yet we are safe, soe it were better to staye till it come," to which he added the grim rejoinder: "It is like that this consideration made the Churches beyonde the seas (as the Palatinate, Rochell etc.) to sitt still at home, and not look out for shelter while they might have found it." The fact that so many of the ministers approved of the New England enterprise he felt to be a reliable sign of its acceptability to God, for surely God would not "seduce his people by his owne prophetts" to follow a course contrary to His will.

The Puritan clergy were also concerned about the infection of the younger generation by the contagious wickedness that surrounded them in England. "The fountains of learninge and religion are so corrupted," wrote Winthrop, "that most Children even the best wittes and of fayrest hopes, are perverted corrupted and utterly overthrowne by the multitude of evill examples and the licentious government of those seminaryes." Nowhere in the numerous drafts of Winthrop's arguments was a denial or an objection raised to this reason for emigration. Winthrop was apparently not the only Puritan father with a wayward son.

America offered many advantages over England; it was folly to sit still and wait the harvest of wrath that other men had sown. But one other thought kept recurring to Winthrop, a gnawing doubt not easily downed: would it not be deserting the world and one's fellow sinners to flee into a brave new land? Though one professed affection for all the saints and all the true churches of England, was it not in fact an act of separation to put three thousand miles of water between oneself and them? Though there might be opportunities to serve the Lord in New England, was it not a duty, especially for a man of some prominence, a justice of the peace, say, to stay in England and keep on striving to bring righteousness there?

This was the question that troubled Winthrop most, and he posed it plainly: "It wilbe a great wronge to our owne Churche and Countrye to take awaye the good people, and we shall laye it the more open to the Judgment feared." Other Puritans felt the objection strongly too, and applied it closely to Winthrop, who was becoming a more important man to the Puritan cause than he may himself have realized. Robert Ryece, a well-known Suffolk antiquary and one of the many friends whom Winthrop consulted, told him bluntly, "The church and common welthe heere at home, hath more neede of your best abyllitie in these dangerous tymes, than any remote plantation."

In his first attempt, Winthrop was unable to answer this objection to his own complete satisfaction. He minimized the number of people involved: those who went would be few, as nothing by comparison with those left behind. Many served no public function in England. Besides, the church of Christ ought to be considered universal, without respect to countries, and it would be a good thing to convert the Indians. These were weak arguments, as he must have known, for he drew up another list, designed to prove "that persons of good use here (yea in publike service) may be transplanted for the furtherance of this plantation in New England."

Though Winthrop's own capacities for public service had hitherto been demonstrated only in local and minor offices, though he had never sat in Parliament, those who knew him evidently recognized that he had extraordinary talents. The members of the Massachusetts Bay Company in particular set their hearts on persuading him to join them, and the new list probably embodied the arguments they advanced to convince him that his services would be more acceptable to God in Massachusetts than in England. The line of reasoning this time was persuasive. The work of planting a godly colony in New England was acknowledged by all to be lawful and honorable. To ensure success, men of ability must engage in it. Probably few would feel inclined to do so, and therefore those with an inclination should also feel an obligation to go. In any case it was better to raise a new church where one did not exist than to labor to better part of an old one. Moreover, a lesser public office might lawfully be deserted for a larger one in another place. Finally, it might be a greater service to the churches of England to preserve a remnant pure in the wilderness than to strive in vain for purity at home. In better times the remnant could expand and extend itself back to the mother country. "It was a good service to the Churche of the Jewes that Joseph and Marye forsooke them, that their mesiah might be preserved for them against tymes of better service." As Winthrop struggled to get over his most difficult moral hurdle, these last two arguments gave him confidence.

His friends in the Bay Company could press the argument of lesser and greater public offices by assuring him that in New England important men would be few, and he would certainly have a leading hand in public affairs, whereas in England his role was minor and likely to become more so in consequence of his dwindling estate. Three of his sons had come of age, and he had launched them with gifts of land that left his own holdings shrunk to half their former size. He would thus no longer be so important a man in the county and would therefore not be appointed to the public offices he could otherwise expect, "and so if he should refuse this opportunitye, that talent, which God hathe bestowed upon him for publike service, were like to be buried." In the margin he phrased it more pungently: "When a man is to wade throughe a deepe water, there is required tallnesse, as well as Courage, and if he findes it past his depth, and God open a gapp another waye, he may take it." Winthrop knew that in England he was not tall enough to do anything effective for the cause of God against the towering ungodliness of King Charles, but in New England Charles would cast a small shadow indeed, and Winthrop would be the giant.

Winthrop did not aim at power for the sake of power, but he longed to use his talents in the cause of God. Massachusetts, his friends in the Bay Company assured him, was the place to do so. The colony was to be a refuge for truth, a religious rather than a commercial enterprise. To attract godly settlers was the main concern, and Winthrop could not deny the argument that, if men who were "knowne to be godly and live in wealthe and prosperity heere, shall forsake all this" to participate in the emigration, their presence would go far to convince the right kind of people that the enterprise was what it purported to be. Winthrop did not doubt the sincerity of his friends in the Bay Company, but they were, after all, only members of the company and could not with authority speak for the whole. The other members might be too shrewd to gainsay the godly motive, which was "such a bewtifull pretexte" that it furnished the answer to all objections. This was the comment of Robert Ryece, who was suspicious of the whole business. "The pipe goeth sweete," he warned Winthrop, "tyll the Byrde be in the nett, many bewtifull hopes are sett before your eyes to allewer you to danger."

What guarantee could there be that the suspicions of Ryece were unwarranted? What if godly settlers failed to be attracted? Or if, after they got to America, the weakling relative or favorite of some influential company official were sent to misrule them and perhaps wreck the whole venture? And if the new colony proved financially unsuccessful, what was to prevent the Massachusetts Bay Company from pulling out and leaving the settlers holding the bag? These were disturbing questions; but a complete and daring answer was already in preparation.

IV

The Way to a New England

Winthrop was in close communication with the leaders of the Massachusetts Bay Company throughout the weeks when he was trying to make up his mind. On July 28, 1629, he and several other prominent Puritans who were interested in emigrating assembled in Lincolnshire to talk it over. They met at Tattershall, the home of Isaac Johnson and his wife the Lady Arbella. Johnson was a member of the company, himself planning to emigrate, and one of those most intimately concerned with trying to enlist Winthrop in the enterprise. He had summoned the meeting to discuss a plan for the government of the colony, a plan so extraordinary that it swept away Winthrop's last doubts.

The Massachusetts Bay Company was a trading corporation with powers of ownership and government over a specified area. There were other such corporations in England with powers over other areas. All held their meetings at London or Plymouth or whatever other English city had been assigned in their charters, and sent governors to carry out their orders in their respective domains across the seas. When the Massachusetts Bay Company obtained its charter, the King and his advisers undoubtedly assumed that it would hold its meetings in London, and so presumably did the members of the company. But through oversight, design, or indifference, no place of meeting was prescribed. It was now proposed to take advantage of the omission by moving the place of meeting to the colony itself. In this way the governor of the company could become himself the governor of the colony, and the general court of the company could become the legislative assembly of the colony.

This daring proposal would effectively remove the colony from control by the Crown. The governmental powers of the company were extensive, greater in many ways then those which the King exercised in England. But as long as the company held its meetings in England, the King and his ministers could easily keep the members under surveillance. If they got too far out of line, as the Virginia Company of London had, they might forfeit their charter, and the King might take over the government of the colony. But if the company moved lock, stock, and barrel to the New World, who would ever know what they were up to?

The advantages of such a move to the Puritans who composed the majority of the membership were obvious. If the company moved to New England, it could become in effect a self-governing commonwealth, with the charter a blank check justifying everything it did. It would thus be able to enforce the laws of God and win divine favor. It could create in New England the kind of society that God demanded of all His servants but that none had yet given Him. The colony would not be a mere commercial enterprise, nor would it be simply a hiding place from the wrath of God. It would be instead the citadel of God's chosen people, a spearhead of world Protestantism.

To be part of such a holy enterprise would justify a man in casting off larger responsibilities than those of a justice of the peace. And it was made clear to Winthrop that his part in the venture would be a crucial one. For two weeks he remained in Lincolnshire, while Johnson and others impressed upon him the extraordinary opportunity and the urgency of his participation. In the end he was forced to admit (speaking in the third person), "It is come to that Issue as (in all probabilitye) the wellfare of the Plantation dependes upon his goeinge, for divers of the Cheife undertakers (upon whom the reste depende) will not goe without him." He could hesitate no longer. On August 26 he rode to Cambridge, where he with eleven other leading Puritans signed an agreement to be ready by the following March to embark for New England, provided that "before the last of September next the whole governement together with the Patent for the said plantacion bee first by an order of Court legally transferred and established to remayne with us and others which shall inhabite upon the said plantacion."

Matthew Cradock, the governor of the company, had meanwhile officially informed the members of the proposal, and on August 29 they met to consider it. Seven of those who had participated in the Cambridge agreement were on hand to press for acceptance. Some members, who had no intention of going to the colony themselves, were reluctant to let their controlling reins slip free, but enough were moved by the arguments of the Cambridge group so that when the question was finally put, "it appeared by the generall consent of the Company, that the government and pattent should bee setled in New England."

Winthrop was thus committed to his decision. The recognition that he must live in the world had led him to the paradoxical conclusion that he should withdraw from the only part of the world he had ever known. Having learned to use the good things that God gave man, he had reached out to strike down the evils that God forbade, and in so doing found that he must save not merely Groton or Suffolk County but England herself. And now he had determined to reach still farther: England, for the moment, could not be saved in England, and perhaps could not be saved at all. The only hope was to cross the water and establish a government of Christ in exile.

The next six months were hectic ones. Before sailing he must put all his affairs in order, transform into the unstable currency of the day the lands which he and his father and grandfather had so painfully acquired, prepare to leave, perhaps forever, the manor where every corner, every tree, every hollow in the ground was as familiar as his own hand. He had learned his Puritan lessons well, and he never set down what it cost him in heartache to put this good part of the world behind him. He did not attempt to conceal, however, what it meant to leave Margaret, even for a short time.

For a while he thought of taking her with him on the first voyage, but when she and Henry's wife both became pregnant, it seemed best that they wait out their time in England. Samuel, Margaret's two-year-old, would stay with them. So would Forth, who was about to be married, and John, Jr., whom Winthrop deputed to conclude the family business and keep the colonists supplied during the first year. John, Jr., had inherited his father's strength of character, and Winthrop was happy to have him at his back. He knew too that John would take good care of Margaret. She was disheartened by the prospect of their separation. As he hurried about his preparations for departure, he dashed off brief letters to cheer her and calm her anxiety about his own safety. "My dear wife," he would write, "be of good courage, it shall go well with thee and us . . . therefore rayse up thy thoughts, and be merrye in the Lorde."

Winthrop had little time for his family in these last months. While winding up his personal affairs he suddenly found the direction of the whole New England enterprise thrust upon him. He had anticipated that he would have a leading role in New England, and when the company decided to transfer the government and charter to New England, he knew that some member who was going there would be elected governor. But he seems not to have expected that he would be the man, even though he was by now a member of the company and therefore eligible for the office. On October 20, 1629, the General Court of the Massachusetts Bay Company (the title of the meeting of members), after nominating four candidates for governor, Winthrop, John Humfrey, Isaac Johnson, and Sir Richard Saltonstall, picked Winthrop by "a generall vote and full consent." "So it is," he wrote his wife, "that [it] hath pleased the Lorde to call me to a further trust in this business of the plantation, than either I expected or finde my selfe fitt for." This at least assured him that he had been right in thinking he would find a more active employment of his talents in the New England venture than at home, but it also meant a great deal of unexpected work to be done before sailing. He must now take charge of the arrangements for the whole expedition: ships, provisions, and passengers.

Of the three, the last was the most difficult task. Winthrop had already started to drum up settlers before he became governor. As soon as he returned from Tattershall with his own mind made up, he set to work on the local prospects. He also committed to paper the arguments and answers to objections which had for weeks been piling up in his own mind. These passed from hand to hand in prominent Puritan circles, where the main campaign was conducted. There were, however, many non-Puritans who were eager to join the godly expedition for economic reasons. It was Winthrop's privilege to reject unsuitable applicants, but it was also his responsibility to see the colony supplied with men trained in all the trades necessary to its success. However desirable it was to have none but godly settlers, if the passenger list lacked a necessary sawyer, cooper, surgeon, or whatever, he must supply one somehow. Much of his time went to sifting letters of recommendation, searching out suitable men with suitable trades, and arranging sponsors to pay the passage of those who could not pay their own. It was generally possible to find someone who would pay the fare of the skilled but poor, and give them bed and board for a specified number of years in return for their services. Settlers who could afford it carried a number of these servants with them, and some of the most essential craftsmen were doubtless transported at the company's expense. Winthrop himself brought at least four entire families and probably more as part of his own household.

While putting together and equipping and financing his expedition, Winthrop had to deal with a problem created by the transformation of a trading company into a holy experiment. The Massachusetts Bay Company had attracted many stockholders who did not wish to adventure their lives along with their money in the New World. The problem was to furnish these less ardent souls with some return on their investment. An agreement was finally worked out whereby the remaining resources of the company would be managed for seven years by "undertakers"—five in England, five in Massachusetts—the profits to be distributed at the end of the period. Long before the seven years were up, it became apparent that there would be no profits. Nevertheless, though the Massachusetts Bay Company, like most colonizing companies, did not prove a sound business investment, probably most of the men who footed the bill did not count the money as wholly lost.

Winthrop's difficulties as governor, even while still in England, were not entirely financial and managerial. As preparations went forward, people all over England talked about the venture. A thousand men and women were selling their possessions and saying good-bye to their friends. Since most of them were Puritans, it was easy to infer that they were Separatists, come-outers who had decided at last to repudiate and defy both England and her churches. Winthrop and his friends were very sensitive to the charge. They were painfully aware that to all appearances they were walking out of a difficult situation. They were sure that they were acting in the best interests of those who remained behind, that the pure church they intended to establish in New England would someday, somehow, rescue its English parent from the mire of corruption. But the fact that their action looked like desertion worried them far more than the dangers they would face in a wilderness. It gave them a half-recognized sense of guilt that cropped out occasionally in unexpected ways. Thomas Shepard, who became one of New England's most eminent ministers and a pillar of strength to Winthrop during a subsequent crisis, later confessed he was all but overcome when his first attempt to leave England was thwarted by stormy seas: "The Lord made me feare my affliction came in part for running too far in a way of separation from the mixt Assemblies in England: tho I blesse God I have ever beeleved that there are true churches in many parishes in England where the Lord sets up able men and ministers of his gospell; and I have abhorred to refuse to heare any able minister in England." Another minister, George Phillips, who lived near Groton and accompanied Winthrop to New England, was so obsessed with the need for avoiding separatism, so determined to avow his participation in the world with all its sins, that he declared not only the churches of England but also those of Rome to be true churches.

Such feelings did not prevent Phillips from leaving his own church for a purer one in the New World. But they made him and many other leaders of New England highly sensitive to any suggestion of schism from the Church of England. The founders were so dazzled by the godly purpose and unique opportunity of their mission in the wilderness that they could not acknowledge their departure from England as in fact a separation. They felt bound to protest too often and too loudly that it was no such thing. Before they left, John Cotton, the brilliant young minister of Boston in Lincolnshire, came down to Southampton and preached them a sermon reassuring them that they had a clear call from God for the work they had undertaken. But in order to reaffirm to their countrymen that they were not religious snobs, bent on demonstrating superior holiness, they published a statement avowing their great affection for the Church of England. They were not, they insisted, Separatists. They were not "of those that dreame of perfection in this world." They did not disavow their membership in the Church of England. "We desire," they told their countrymen, "you would be pleased to take notice of the principals, and body of our company, as those who esteeme it our honour, to call the Church of England, from whence wee rise, our deare Mother, and cannot part from our native Country, where she specially resideth, without much sadnes of heart, and many teares in our eyes, ever acknowledging that such hope and part as wee have obtained in the common salvation, we have received in her bosome, and suckt it from her breasts." It was an eloquent statement, a little too eloquent, but all the more deeply felt because of the facts that seemed to belie it.

Winthrop and his friends issued their statement from aboard the *Arbella,* the flagship of the expedition, on April 7, 1630, and the next day the ship was under way. Across the receding water his thoughts reached confidently back to Margaret. They had made an agreement to think of each other every Monday and Friday between five and six o'clock and so hold communion together. As soon as possible she would join him. "Oh how it refresheth my heart," he wrote to her, "to thinke that I shall yet againe see thy sweet face in the lande of the livinge, that lovely countenance that I have so much delighted in, and beheld with so great contente!"

And in the other direction, still more insistent, lay the vision of a new England.

V

Survival

April and May were cold in the North Atlantic; the sun did not seem to have the warmth it did in England. As the ship rolled and pitched and groaned through heavy gales, the landlubbers packed below groaned too. Winthrop routed them out periodically and set them playing games on deck, where fresh air and salt spray revived lagging spirits. But two months of heavy seas and spare diet had wearied everyone by the time land was sighted off Cape Sable on June 6. Two days later they got their first glimpse of New England: the hills of Mount Desert. It was a fair day, with a fresh, clear breeze bearing the fragrance of a million fir trees, "and there came a smell off the shore like the smell of a garden."

For the next three days the ship cruised west and south across the Gulf of Maine, sometimes tacking in close enough so that the passengers could make out the trees along the shore, then out again and away, with that sweet smell of land lingering in the nostrils. Once they caught the outline of the White Mountains in the distance. On June 11 they passed the Isles of Shoals, where a ship lay at anchor and five or six fishing shallops bobbed merrily up and down. They were in sight of Cape Ann before dark and stood toward it against a southwest gale, finally rounding the point about sunrise the next morning. Wind and tide were with them now, and while curious eyes looked out from Salem harbor, the *Arbella* sailed through the channel between Bakers Island and Little Island and cast anchor about ten o'clock off Plum Cove.

As the sea-weary company of men and women looked ashore at the straggling collection of huts and hovels and canvas booths that went by the name of Salem, they must have been staggered by the crudity of the life that lay ahead of them. The land was lovely but savage. Only a few hundred acres were cleared; beyond lay the forest, and they had seen for themselves how the huge trees came down to the shore along the coast to the north and east. How was this land to support them through the coming winter? Four hundred men, women, and children had come on the *Arbella* and the three ships that accompanied her. Six hundred more were on the way. Some had brought supplies to last until next season, but many poor families had pressed aboard at the last minute with little but zeal for provision. These would now look pitifully to the others for bread, and even the best prepared had little to spare. It cost the better part of fifty pounds to come to New England properly equipped, even if one knew exactly what to bring and what not to bring. And much was lost on the way. The most skillfully packed hogsheads of meal were not proof against the North Atlantic.

At best, to live for a year on the kind of food that could be salted and dried and put up was to invite scurvy. Though it was understood that lemon and lime juice were good preventives, they were not easily come by, and many put their faith in quack remedies instead. Fresh meat would have helped more than anything else, but it cost fifteen pounds merely for the freight of one cow. To be sure, the woods abounded with game (which must have been unusually plentiful as a result of the plague which had decimated the Indian population of the region twelve or thirteen years before), and the settlers had guns. But the guns were matchlocks, with which a man might conceivably shoot a deer, if he had great familiarity with the weapon and great skill in stalking. There were precious few in the group with such accomplishments. Even the gentlemen of the expedition had had little experience in shooting at game. They had either forsworn it, like Winthrop, or they had followed the more fashionable form of hunting with falcons. Consequently, native game offered little hope, and since it included a large number of wolves, it may have destroyed as much in cattle as it furnished in venison or turkey.

The four hundred hungry, hollow-eyed men and women who stumbled ashore at Salem, many already weak with malnutrition, saw little to renew their strength. The summer heat, hotter than any they had known in England, was debilitating. The settlers who had spent the previous winter there could tell them that the winters were colder, too. How would they shelter themselves in such cold? A few had brought tents, but even a tent cost ten pounds in London. They could be improvised of course, but at best they would make a frail fence against the winter. Many of the old settlers were living in wigwams they had made like the Indians', of saplings stuck in the ground, tied together at the top, and covered with thatch or bark or skins. Inside they built fires and huddled like savages in the smoke that curled up through a hole at the top. They were as weak as the newcomers they greeted. Eighty had died in the preceding winter, and the new arrivals quickly began to add to the number.

That such a settlement could provoke the jealousy of a foreign power was laughable, yet the French and Spanish both had rival colonies in the New World and might at any time attack. Near at hand the Indians, whose cornfields might fill empty bellies, could easily turn from hospitality to hostility. They knew the country much better than the English and knew how to live off it. If they wished, they could easily drive the sickly invaders into the sea.

Looking over the beachhead to which he had brought so large and so weak a force, Winthrop saw that the colony needed backbone. On the faces of the languid men around him he read a failure of nerve. Many were already in the forlorn and lackadaisical state of mind that marks the onset of scurvy. Others, because of their short supplies and their disappointment in the primitive condition of the settlement, were ready to give up.

Little is known about Winthrop's movements during those first few months. He was too busy now to make more than a few scattered entries in the journal he had begun aboard ship. His letters to Margaret were infrequent, and he even admitted that he often failed to think of her at the appointed time on Mondays and Fridays. When he did write, he stressed the need to come well provided, and hurried off letters to young John to the same effect: bring forty hogsheads of meal at least, peas and oatmeal well dried as much as you can, good store of dry Suffolk cheese, sugar and fruit, pepper and ginger, vinegar and verjuice, in good casks and iron-bound. He never suggested that they should think twice about coming. Though his companions were dying, and his son Henry was drowned within a few days of arrival, and scores of his colonists were returning home on the ships that brought them, he seems never to have had a doubt about ultimate success. In his first letter to Margaret, written on July 16, after reciting the various afflictions, he concludes, "Yet for all these thinges (I prayse my God) I am not discouraged, nor doe I see cause to repent, or dispaire of those good dayes heere, which will make amends for all."

A glimpse of the effect of this confidence on the others emerges in a report that was shortly going the rounds in London. So soon "as Mr. Winthrop was landed, perceiving what misery was like to ensewe through theire Idlenes, he presently fell to worke with his owne hands, and thereby soe encouradged the rest that there was not an Idle person then to be found in the whole Plantation and whereas the Indians said they would shortly retorne as fast as they came, now they admired to see in what short time they had all housed themselves and planted Corne sufficient for theire subsistance." Unfortunately, it was not quite that simple.

Winthrop's first move was to look for a roomier place than Salem in which to settle. There was not enough open land there, and the drab surroundings were bad for morale. Three days after landing he was off to explore the bay that lay to the south. He cruised for several miles up the Mystic River and took note of the meadows (Englishmen called them "champion land") with their fat black earth. Coming back, he stopped and spent the night at the fine house which Samuel Maverick had built at the mouth of the river on the north side, all encompassed by a palisade. Here was sufficient proof of what a little effort and courage would do. Maverick, a well-bred young man, had come over with his bride six years before, had built this house and fortified it, and now lived there like a king, offering hospitality to all who came. He seemed to have passed his six years in the wilderness as comfortably and civilly as if he had been in London. If one man could do so well in his own cause, how much more could a thousand do in the cause of God?

Winthrop doubtless surveyed the rest of the bay, including the peninsula of Charlestown, where an outpost of settlers from Salem had encamped the year before and constructed a large frame house. Hurrying back to Salem he passed out of the bay through the ship channel on the south by way of Nantasket (where he found a shipload of settlers deposited by a captain who could not be bothered to convey them farther). He returned with the conclusion that the bay was the place to settle: there was plenty of champion land on its rivers and peninsulas, and the islands which dotted it gave such protection against wind and wave that it was really an inland lake. On the peninsulas, with their narrow necks, it would be easy to keep out wolves and marauding Indians, while the bay itself, though navigable between the islands by small boats of shallow draft, could be entered by ships only through the channel at Nantasket. By commanding that channel he could defend the whole place against attack by Spain or France. There was no point in trying to crowd a thousand people into Salem when this land of Canaan lay waiting. Winthrop packed up the expedition again and landed it at Charlestown. From here the settlers fanned out and soon had plantations stretched around the bay from Dorchester on the south through Roxbury, Watertown, Newtown (Cambridge), and Boston to Charlestown on the north.

Winthrop, making his headquarters at Charlestown, next set about gathering food against the coming winter. The most reliable of the ship captains, Master William Peirce of the *Lyon,* he dispatched to Bristol with a bill of exchange and a letter to John, to see that money was furnished at once to buy provisions. Meanwhile, Winthrop sent men cruising up and down the coast to trade for corn wherever they could find the Indians or settlers willing to sell. One pinnace brought back a hundred bushels from Cape Cod. With the Indians about the bay he dealt personally. His solemnity of manner was precisely the attitude to win their respect, and he took care that relations should be on his terms, not theirs. With that unabashed assumption of superiority which was to carry English rule around the world, he noted of one sachem who visited him with a gift of corn that "being in English clothes, the governour set him at his own table, where he behaved himself as soberly, etc., as an Englishman."

While the governor collected corn, the settlers were digging in, many of them literally. They carved caves in the hillsides and dug cellars which they roofed over. Others constructed wigwams. In this land of too many forests, dressed wood was still at a premium, for Englishmen were sawyers, not axmen, and it took time to rip out boards in a saw pit. Nevertheless, a few frame houses went up in all the settlements. At Charlestown, where Winthrop and the other officers of the company lived in the house constructed the year before, there was much sickness, which the settlers attributed to the water. Charlestown had plenty of water available by wells or ponds, but there was only one small spring, and Englishmen, who considered water to be at best a dubious beverage, thought that only spring water was to be trusted. After Isaac Johnson died on the last day of September—his wife, the Lady Arbella, died a month before him—Winthrop and most of the others in Charlestown crossed over to the peninsula of Boston, bringing with them the frame of a house that Winthrop had begun to erect in Charlestown.

Until then Boston had been the dominion of another of those individuals who found the Old World too small. William Blackstone, like Samuel Maverick across the bay, was a well-educated, sophisticated man who had been living quietly for several years in the country now inundated by saints. It is quite likely that he was acquainted with some of the new arrivals, for he was a Lincolnshireman and a collegemate of Isaac Johnson's at Cambridge. It is even likely that Johnson crossed over and became a neighbor of Blackstone's at Boston (first called Trimountain) before he died. In any case, when the Charlestown settlers decided to find a place with better water, Blackstone showed Winthrop an excellent spring, emptying by a brook into a little cove on the eastern side of the peninsula. Winthrop led the exodus from Charlestown, setting up a dock at the head of the cove (now Dock Square), and here began the town of Boston, which soon was recognized as the political and economic center of the colony.

At Boston and the other plantations around the bay the settlers still sickened and died as they measured out their corn and scoured the rocks at low tide for mussels. "Bread was so very scarce," one of them later remembered, "that sometimes I thought the very crusts of my father's table would have been very sweet unto me. And when I could have meal and water and salt boiled together, it was so good, who could wish better?" Virus and bacteria struck without respect to persons, and by the end of November Winthrop had lost eleven of the servants whom he counted as part of his family, but he was himself still in good health and still confident. "I thanke God," he wrote Margaret in September, "I like so well to be heer, as I doe not repent my comminge: and if I were to come againe, I would not have altered my course, though I had foreseene all these Afflictions: I never fared better in my life, never slept better, never had more content of minde."

Others shared his resolution or caught the infectious spirit of it, else there would have been a larger number of graves in the coming winter and a heavier freight of return passengers in the spring. But few of the settlers were writing home in such terms as he used with Margaret. Most of the letters from Massachusetts that autumn were filled with disillusionment, and before the winter was over, there were tales to tell which would cool the enthusiasm of anyone contemplating a voyage to the New English Canaan. Winter struck first with a freezing northwest gale on the day before Christmas, and thereafter the settlers, unaccustomed to the temperatures, got their hands and feet frozen and sometimes died on short trips undertaken too casually. In their crude huts they built up the fires too large, so that chimneys daubed together out of clay and wood took fire, and so did the highly combustible thatched roofs, with no means at hand to extinguish them.

In February when starvation was in sight, Master Peirce came sailing up the bay in the *Lyon*, freighted with supplies that gladdened every heart, including a good store of lemon juice. A day or two later the cold broke. When Peirce prepared to return, however, he had eighty-odd passengers who had seen enough of New England, and he carried letters calling pitifully for help: "Lovinge fathere thoue I be far disstante from you yet I pray you remembure me as youer cheield and we do not know how longe we may subeseiste for we can not live her witheought provisseyones from ould eingland . . . so father I pray consedre of my cause for her will be but a verey por beinge and no beinge withe ought Lovinge father youer helpe withe provisseyones from ould eingland."

Two hundred had died that winter, and perhaps as many more returned home in the spring. It was a crude winnowing, for some of the most promising men had been lost. Nevertheless, most of those who remained realized that they had seen the worst and were ready to stick it out. Winthrop, as buoyant as ever, wrote to Margaret, "I want nothinge but thee and the rest of my family."

In addition to boosting the morale of the colony, springtime and the resumption of sea traffic brought a new problem for Winthrop. The sad tales told by the returning planters, who doubtless exaggerated their troubles in order to justify their retreat, combined with the discouraging letters from those who stayed, inevitably had their effect in England. In the previous year when the Massachusetts expedition embarked, so large and so full of hope, good Puritan merchants were ready to expect great things of it, and had given glib assurances of their friendship and their intention to send supplies over for sale to the prosperous colonists. Now, with so many deaths, so many hopeful men returning, and the colonists very unprosperous, the host of friends vanished. John Humfrey, one who remained faithful, had begun to take subscriptions for a common stock to send over provisions as soon as the fleet set sail, for he had observed that many were going without enough to carry them through the winter. He easily obtained promises amounting to five hundred pounds. But as reports began to arrive from the colony, money lost heart more quickly than men. The subscribers gave up the whole enterprise as lost and refused to honor their obligations. "When wee least need freindes," Humfrey observed sadly, "possiblie wee may have them to befreind us."

Winthrop dug deep in his own pocket and paid for enough supplies to save the day, but the stay-at-homes did not realize that the day had been saved. Even Humfrey himself and Emmanuel Downing, who were both planning to come to the colony, were much shaken. They still looked to escape the wrath of God in the New World, but they doubted now that New England was the place. Winthrop, who had been exerting himself to prepare a house for Downing, was dismayed to hear from his brother-in-law that "our freindes here, yea those of best Judgement [meaning, among others, himself] wishe you bestowe not much Cost in building where you are, but doe advise that you doe speedily send about the discoverie of some fitter place more to the South." Winthrop received much advice to this effect from men who at the distance of three thousand miles were more afraid of the New England weather than he. There was less snow in the Narragansett country, they told him; and the Hudson River was still better.

Unfortunately, Winthrop's replies have not been preserved. There remains only a letter from Downing expressing his surprise that the colony survived the winter, and one from John, Jr., stating that Uncle Downing was now "well satisfied with your reasons you give him for the Country." Downing may have been satisfied, but he did not come over for seven years, and two years later word still had it in London that the planters in New England were starving and about to come home.

Actually there was never again a starving time in New England like that first winter. As soon as spring came the colonists began planting the champion ground in and around their settlements. Winthrop carved out a farm of six hundred acres on the fat land that had pleased him up the Mystic River and set his large family of servants to cultivating it and building him a stone house. He made periodic visits to inspect his new domain and there tasted the hazardous life of the ordinary pioneer. He never ventured out without a gun in hand, "supposing he might see a wolf, (for they came daily about the house and killed swine and calves . . .)." Getting lost was another common danger, for there were only footpaths through the forest, which lay everywhere within a few hundred feet of a man's door. Winthrop once missed his path half a mile from the house and spent a sleepless night pacing up and down beside his campfire, gathering wood, and singing psalms. For such emergencies he "always carried about him match and a compass, and in summer time snakeweed," which the Indians had taught him to use as a remedy for snakebite.

Winthrop's travels from Boston generally took him to settlements other than his farm and on business other than his own. What occupied him most immediately was the difficult matter of getting the colony on a paying basis. Somehow the country must be made to furnish not only the wherewithal to keep itself alive but also something to pay for the supplies it had to buy from England: clothing, hardware, glass, and a thousand other things. There must be a "staple," some article the colony could produce better and cheaper than other places. In this first year or two there seemed to be several possibilities. One was hemp, for a native hemplike plant looked promising. Another was sassafras, much in demand in the Old World as a cure for syphilis. Wine might be produced from the abundant wild grapes, and some of the swamps held bog iron. But most certain of all were furs and fish.

Both required the use of ships, and Winthrop had had the foresight to bring over a number of skilled ship wrights including William Stephens, who had built a ship of six hundred tons and was said to be so able a man that there was hardly such another to be found in all England. By the fourth of July these men were ready to launch a thirty-ton bark at Mystic, which Winthrop named *The Blessing of the Bay*. When she was rigged, he sent her off to trade for furs along the coast. The next year they built a ship of sixty tons at Medford.

What principally sustained the colony, however, and indeed brought it prosperity during the first ten years of its existence, was neither fish nor fur nor any other staple, but immigrants. For ten years the activities of Charles I and of Bishop Laud filled the sea lanes with ships crowding sail for New England. In spite of the woeful tales about the expiring condition of Massachusetts, God's wrath in England seemed to many a more imminent danger. Before Charles's futile attempt to rule without Parliament ended, between fifteen and twenty thousand people crossed the ocean. The ships that carried them were freighted with window glass and chimney backs, pots and kettles, guns and gunpowder, cloth and clothing, saws and axes, but not fresh food, milk, or boards. In the newcomers therefore, the old settlers found a ready market for the very things that they could most readily produce—dressed lumber, corn, cattle (cattle breeding became a principal occupation in these early years)—and at the same time a source of supply for the things that they themselves needed.

The only problem raised by this economy, so long as the stream of settlers lasted, was to prevent prices and wages from skyrocketing in a dizzy spiral. This was a job for government. In England, as a justice of the peace, Winthrop had doubtless sat in the sessions at Bury St. Edmunds to assign maximum wages for Suffolk workmen in various trades. In Massachusetts, as in England, the sin of charging more than a just wage or price was known as "oppression," and Winthrop and the other leaders of the colony were continually alert to prevent and punish it. At their first official meeting, held at Charlestown on August

23, 1630, maximum wages for carpenters, joiners, brick-layers, sawyers, and thatchers were set at two shillings a day, eightpence more than the justices at Bury, four months earlier, had assigned for the same trades in Suffolk. Later, as ships began to bring over large quantities of English goods, it was ordered that these should not be sold for more than fourpence in the shilling above what they cost in England. Unhappily the law of supply and demand proved stronger than the General Court, and in 1636 the problem was turned over to the towns. There was no easy solution. Oppression continued to be a problem in Massachusetts throughout the seventeenth century: but the efforts of the authorities to keep it in check were by no means perfunctory, and saved Massachusetts from the runaway prices that plagued later Americans in frontier boom towns.

By the fall of 1631, when Margaret and the rest of his family arrived, Winthrop knew that he no longer need worry excessively about the simple problem of survival. As Margaret came ashore with volleys of shot, people from all over the colony came to welcome her, and for days, in gratitude and respect for her husband, they sent gifts of "fat hogs, kids, venison, poultry, geese, partridges, etc., so as the like joy and manifestation of love had never been seen in New England. It was a great marvel, that so much people and such store of provisions could be gathered together at so few hours' warning."

It was a great marvel truly enough. It was also a great personal triumph for Winthrop. Under his guidance these people had left starvation behind. The Lord had pleased to give them all full bellies and a roof against the rain. The Lord had pleased to place Margaret once more by his side. Who could ask for greater proof that the Lord was pleased with His servant and with the people who had entered this wilderness to worship Him? It was up to them all now to justify His pleasure.

VI

A Special Commission

To please God the Puritans demanded of themselves a standard of behavior not far different from that required by most modern codes of morality. They did not think it necessary to be either prudes or prohibitionists. They did not dress in drab clothes or live in drab houses or speak in drab words. The people who appear in the pages of Winthrop's journal, the good men and women who showered him with venison and partridges and fat hogs to celebrate Margaret's arrival, the boys and girls who skipped rope on the decks of the *Arbella,* the men who built ships and caught fish and planted corn were all human enough.

Nevertheless, the Puritans did make strong demands on human nature, for they were engaged in a mission that required great exertion. They had undertaken to establish a society where the will of God would be observed in every detail, a kingdom of God on earth. While still aboard the *Arbella,* Winthrop had explained to his fellow emigrants their solemn commitment to this task. Every nation, they all knew, existed by virtue of a covenant with God in which it promised to obey His commands. They had left England because England was failing in its promise. In high hope that God was guiding them and would find their efforts acceptable, they had proposed to form a new society. Now God had demonstrated His approval. He had made way for them by a "special overruling providence."

By staying His wrath so long and allowing them to depart in peace, by delivering them safe across the water, He had sealed a covenant with them and given them a special responsibility to carry out the good intentions that had brought them into the wilderness. Theirs was a special commission. And "when God gives a special Commission," Winthrop warned them, "He lookes to have it stricktly observed in every Article."

All must therefore work together to attain the end of their coming. They must not allow any selfish private motives to interfere with their plan, for though every society must make its covenant with God, they had been singled out, like Israel of old, to serve as a model for others. They would be a city set on a hill: "the eies of all people are uppon us; soe that if wee shall deal falsely with our god in this worke wee have undertaken and soe cause him to withdrawe his present help from us, wee shall be made a story and a by-word through the world, wee shall open the mouthes of enemies to speake evill of the wayes of god and all professours for Gods sake; wee shall shame the faces of many of gods worthy servants, and cause theire prayers to be turned into Cursses upon us till wee be consumed out of the good land whither wee are goeing."

Winthrop was determined that Massachusetts should not deal falsely with God. Before arriving in New England, he and the other leaders of the exodus had thought long and hard about the articles of God's special commission, and they were confident that they knew what was required of them. They knew, in the most elementary terms, that they must punish every sin committed in Massachusetts. And punish they did, with the eager cooperation of the whole community, who knew that sin unpunished might expose them all to the wrath of God. Families became little cells of righteousness where the mother and father disciplined not only their children but also their servants and any boarders they might take in. In order that no one should escape this wholesome control, it was forbidden for anyone to live alone: unmarried men and maids were required to place themselves in some family if their own had been left behind. Parents were obliged to take care that all their children and apprentices learned to read, so that everyone would be able to see for himself in the Bible what opportunities for salvation God offered to man and what sins He forbade. The churches were thronged every Sunday with willing and unwilling worshipers—everyone was required to attend—and church members guarded each other's morals by censuring or excommunicating those who strayed from the straight path.

With virtually the whole population for a police force Winthrop found it no problem to punish sin. It was sometimes difficult, however, to determine exactly what was sinful and what was not. The grosser forms of sin were easily identified. Among the emigrants were men—and women too—who stole and fought and made love without a marriage contract and cursed their betters with primeval eloquence. In these cheerful practitioners sin wore obvious labels. But some cases were not so clear. The line between sin and mere temptation or between sin and simple human pleasure was often a thin one. Yet Winthrop knew that that line must be firmly drawn, for it would be as wrong to forbid what God allowed as it would be to allow what He forbade.

How easy it was to err and how earnestly the Puritans sought to avoid error may be seen in their treatment of the problem of alcohol. The Puritans did not make the simple mistake of condemning all use of alcohol. Liquor was one of the good things that God had furnished His people for their comfort, nourishment, and recreation. Drunkenness, however, was wrong, and the Puritans punished it without hesitation. But the path from drink to drunkenness was so short and easy that they found it hard to decide whether any barriers should be placed along it. Since the path seemed to be even shorter for Indians than for English-men, the authorities at one time forbade the sale of all liquors to them but later relented on the ground that it was "not fit to deprive the Indians of any lawfull comfort which God aloweth to all men by the use of wine." For themselves the closest the Puritans came to a self-denying ordinance was a law forbidding people to drink toasts to one another. In passing it they hoped to prevent drunken-ness, quarreling, bloodshed, uncleanness, misuse of pre-cious time—and the waste of wine and beer.

Here, in spite of the appeal to frugality, they went be-yond the terms of God's commission, for they were forbid-ding a temptation rather than a sin. Winthrop's friend and adviser Thomas Shepard, the respected minister of the church at Cambridge, pointed out the defection. The law, said Shepard in a letter to Winthrop, was all wrong. By treating a temptation as a sin, it would provoke God, for this was making "more sins than (as yet is seene) God himselfe hath made."

In general Winthrop avoided such errors of judgment himself. But many men who had not learned the lesson he had were determined to set up more sins than God did, be-cause they did not know the limits of man's ability and of God's commands. These well-meaning zealots failed to rec-ognize that God's kingdom on earth must still be a king-dom of flesh and blood, and their misdirected zeal soon in-dicated to Winthrop that he faced a far more difficult problem to control the good than to punish the wicked.

The authorities in England, of course, had a way of handling the problem of fanatics: bore their tongues, cut off their ears, brand them, imprison them, silence them. Though all these methods were ultimately used in Massa-chusetts, they did not commend themselves to anyone with Winthrop's political sense. The result of their use in England was not the suppression but the multiplication of fanatics, who swarmed out of the country to Holland and to New England. (They did not leave as fast as they multiplied, however, and in ten years' time rose up to overwhelm their oppressors.)

In Massachusetts Winthrop had no intention of making the mistakes that King Charles and Bishop Laud were making in England. He welcomed all Puritans who fled from the mother country. Every ship that arrived in Boston carried its cargo of them, simple men and women for the most part, who had come with much the same purpose in mind that he had, people who had learned not to aim higher than God demanded, and not lower, either. But among them was a liberal proportion of those who did aim too high.

Some were Separatists, men who had renounced the Church of England and proposed to live and worship in unblemished purity in the New World. Theirs was the position that Winthrop and his friends had expressly disavowed in the statement issued aboard the *Arbella* before departure. Others, while not separatist in name (because they failed to repudiate the Anglican Church), were nevertheless separatist by nature. They too looked for perfection in this world and had come to New England to be right while the rest of the world went wrong.

This separatist impulse was probably present to some degree in most settlers. The men who came to New England had shown, by so doing, that they were unwilling to tolerate evils that other men found tolerable. They had burned their bridges; they had lost whatever they had to lose through intransigence, and they were in consequence all the more ready to insist on their opinions, all the more reluctant to compromise. Some of them had stood before Bishop Laud and defied him. Would they hesitate to defy John Winthrop or anyone else who ventured to disagree with them?

To construct a commonwealth of such persons, a commonwealth "wherin the least known evils are not to bee tollerated," was a delicate task. Their constant demand for purity threatened in several ways the success of Winthrop's mission to the wilderness. Not only did they seek to read into the commission articles which God, in Winthrop's view at least, had not put there, but when their extravagant demands were not met, they threatened to disrupt the colony. The Separatist was always ready to disagree with his neighbors and, when they failed to meet his standards, to withdraw into a lofty and querulous independence, accompanied by all whom he could persuade to join him. In a population so heavily burdened with principles as that of Massachusetts, the danger of such withdrawals was constant. And if the process once began, there was no telling where it would stop. Separatism might splinter the colony into a hundred earnest little Utopias, each feeding on its own special type of holiness and each breeding new types, multiplying, like earthworms, by division. Separatists could disintegrate the colony and dissolve its special commission.

Separatism posed another, external danger when it reached the point of repudiating the churches of England. Winthrop and most of his colleagues thought that such a repudiation would be wrong in itself, a failure of charity, an arrogation of too exclusive a righteousness. But it would also be a danger to the execution of the colony's special commission, because it might excite the anger of the English Government. If the King and his bishops heard that Massachusetts disavowed the Church of England, they might revoke the charter and put an end to the whole experiment.

This was a danger not easily met. It was impossible to censor every letter sent home, and jubilant Puritans frequently wrote back in gloating terms about the purity of their churches by comparison with the corruption of England. "You that are under lee I hope forgett us not that are yett in the storme," an English friend wrote apprehensively to Winthrop, but too many New Englanders remembered their friends in England only to vaunt it over them. Occasionally individuals would return to the mother country to settle unfinished business, and these first innocents abroad proved quite as insufferable in their claims of superior holiness as later generations in their claims of superior plumbing. As a result the colony was in continual danger of interference from England.

The history of Massachusetts during Winthrop's lifetime is very largely the history of his efforts to meet the various dangers presented by separatism. No one could have been better equipped for the task, for Winthrop was obliged to do for Massachusetts precisely what he had already done for himself. He had learned not to avoid but to face temptations, not to spurn the good things that God had given him; even so he must restrain the overzealous from setting for the community a standard of godliness that would deny the humanity of human beings. He had learned not to expect perfection in this world, and to march in company with other sinners, for sin, though it must be punished, could not be stamped out. Even so he must temper the zeal of the Separatists and prevent them from splitting the community or leading it in search of impossible goals.

His success in suppressing the separatist impulse within himself was good reason for supposing that he might suppress it in Massachusetts. But he could not have foreseen how much more powerful a force separatism would prove in New England than it had in old.

In England the focal point of Puritan irritation had always been the church, and in Massachusetts the most important requirement of the colony's special commission, everyone agreed, was the establishment of churches organized precisely as God commanded. English Puritans had considered this crucial matter for three generations but had never been able to agree on what precisely God did command. They all knew there must be an end to bishops and archbishops, an end to the idolatrous ritual and trappings that exalted the clergy instead of God in the divine service, but they disagreed about two important matters.

One group, known as Presbyterians, insisted that the bishops be replaced by another organization, with churches and clergy arranged in a pyramidal structure: groups of churches would be formed into presbyteries, presbyteries into synods, and these collective bodies would exercise a supervisory control over their members. The other Puritans, who ultimately took the name of Congregationalists, had a simpler plan: destroy the bishops and then let each individual church, each congregation, be sufficient to itself. There was, they said, no church larger than a congregation.

The second point on which Presbyterians and Congregationalists differed was the composition of the church. The Presbyterians wished to continue the practice of admitting to membership and to the sacraments everyone who did not forefeit the privilege by some scandalously sinful behavior. The Congregationalists, on the other hand, insisted that membership be confined to persons who could prove, beyond a reasonable doubt, that they had been singled out by God for salvation. It was possible to tell who was a saint, they thought, even in this world, and while everyone must be made to attend church, only the saints should be admitted to membership.

The Congregationalists thus wished to make more sweeping changes than the Presbyterians. Some of them were so impatient with the Church of England that they did not wait for the opportunity to change it but simply withdrew and formed their own churches. These were the Separatists already noticed. Restriction of membership and local independence made it possible to begin a Congregational church anywhere that a handful of saints could be gathered for the purpose. Indeed, one of the men who first expounded the system called it "reformation without tarrying for any," a phrase which adequately states the aim of separatists in all ages.

In the mass migration of the 1630's many Separatists came and doubtless many Presbyterians, but the leaders and probably the majority of immigrants were Congregationalists who had declined to repudiate the English churches. Because they had refused to separate, they had had no previous practical experience in the operation of congregationalism and, with a very few exceptions, knew it only from books. Winthrop, for example, had been the patron of the church at Groton, with power to appoint the minister there. It is possible that he allowed the congregation to make the choice, according to Congregational precept, and it is likely that the Groton church was very lax about conforming to the prescribed rituals of the Church of England, but there could have been no exclusion of the unregenerate from membership. Consequently, neither Winthrop nor any of the other Puritans, who came from similar situations, could have appreciated in advance what forces would be released and what problems created by the wholesale practice of Congregationalism.

The first church within the boundaries of Massachusetts Bay to be founded in the congregational manner was "gathered" (the term usually employed) on July 20, 1629, at Salem by the settlers sent out under Endecott. As the great wave of men and women arrived the following year, they followed the instructions in their books and gathered churches as rapidly as they dug themselves in. By 1635 a dozen churches were scattered round the bay from Hingham to Newbury.

At its beginning a church contained only a handful of members. Usually it was thought proper to start with at least seven, though at Charlestown there were only four. The first members chose a minister and began the process of sifting the population of their town, or "plantation," to find the saints. In England a reputation for godliness and the willingness to join in a church forbidden by law had probably been sufficient evidence of sainthood. But in Massachusetts, with no bishop on hand to threaten the proceedings, churches became more choosy. Candidates were now obliged to describe their inward spiritual experiences, how they reached the moment of conversion, and how their subsequent lives had exhibited its effects. If they passed this examination, they were allowed to subscribe the church covenant, by which they agreed to join with the other members in worship and holy living. Having done so, they then participated in the judgment of future candidates. Generally a unanimous consent was required for every admission.

For ten years the human flood swept into Massachusetts, pushing up the rivers, swarming over the champion lands, some twenty thousand souls, and every soul was checked off as saved or damned. The effect on those who failed to make the grade is difficult to calculate. Some were doubtless conscientious Puritans who simply never felt the moving of grace in their souls and did not want admission without it. Others may have been hardened sinners who scorned admission on any terms, men who could wield a hammer and a spade and a tankard and curse the godly with a free heart. Whoever they were they made surprisingly few complaints about exclusion from the privileges of church membership.

The effect on the saints, however, was profound. They were required continually to pass judgment of the most dreadful kind on their fellow men. They must search not only their own souls for signs of grace, but also the souls of their neighbors. As they gathered together in their pure churches, placing the mark of holiness on their own foreheads and of damnation on most of their neighbors, the experience could not fail to induce that intellectual arrogance which is the breeder of separatism. Though in England they had denounced the evils of separation, the very act of forming a Congregational church necessitated an assumption of superior purity and thereby encouraged a separatist frame of mind. Never in American history did a community produce separatists more attractive or more dangerous than those of early Massachusetts.

What made them dangerous was that the Congregationalism which propagated them also blocked the most obvious means of controlling them. Both in the Church of England and in the Presbyterian system a central organization could police the orthodoxy of individual churches. Congregationalism allowed no central organization: every church was independent. Thus while one distinctive feature of Congregationalism, regenerate membership, encouraged separatism, another feature, congregational autonomy, destroyed the most effective method of control. The people of Massachusetts had in fact undertaken an almost impossible task: they had accepted a commission which required them to follow a specific body of religious principles; but among those principles was one which encouraged the development of schism and another which denied them the means of preventing it.

The Puritans tried always to rest their religious principles, like their social, political, legal, and moral ones, on the Bible, the infallible guidebook for establishing a kingdom of God on earth. But the Bible, while it spoke with unquestioned authority, said different things to different people. To some it seemed to prescribe Presbyterianism, to others Congregationalism, and to different Congregationalists it said different things about baptism or sanctification or communion. The Congregationalists who founded New England were pretty well agreed on what it said about most matters, but among so many earnest students of the Bible, there was always one to discover a new and heretical meaning in a familiar passage and to demand

that everyone else accept it. More often than not the inno-
vator was a minister who used his pulpit to persuade his
congregation, and the separatist impulse would soon be
threatening to split that congregation away from the rest
of the colony. With congregational independence recognized as a fundamental principle, what was to prevent it?

Fortunately, reason could heal differences as well as create them, and the Puritans were extraordinarily reasonable men. The zeal with which they studied the Bible
sprang from supreme confidence in the ability of reason to
find the truth there. Not knowledge but ignorance, they
believed, was the mother of heresy. Therefore they listened
with respect to everyone who could give reasons for an
opinion, and if they thought the reasons faulty, they used
every possible argument to show why. The paper relics of
their contests have survived: the arguments and the answers to arguments and the replies to the answers and the
answers to the replies to the answers, all loaded with
scriptural citations. It was a tedious process, but usually it
worked, because these people feared to err and took each
other seriously.

Because they were so reasonable they were also able to
do much by informal methods. The clergy were all learned
men, skilled in marshaling arguments, and enjoyed therefore a social and intellectual prestige that enabled them to
exert a powerful influence among their people—so powerful that New England Congregationalism came to be
known as a speaking aristocracy in the face of a silent
democracy. Though they were excluded from authority
beyond their respective congregations, the handicaps of
congregational independence were minimized when the
ministers of a particular locality began meeting together in
"consociations" to thrash out disagreements. If the ministers could agree, the congregations would be likely to.
When an especially difficult problem arose, it was possible
to call a synod, not of course the Presbyterian type of

synod with authority to establish its findings, but a Congregational synod, which was simply a full meeting of the colony's ministers, whose findings had no more authority than the report of a committee of experts called in for consultation. No individual or church was obliged to abide by the report, but most pious men and women would hesitate to back their own views above the collective wisdom of the clergy.

Much could be done by such indirect methods to keep individuals and churches from flying off on separatist tangents. But in the end there had to be some tribunal, some court of last resort, to deal with the man or woman or church that had gone too far in separatism to listen to argument. Since each congregation could rightfully claim an absolute independence of the others, such a tribunal could not lie with the churches or with their clergy. But what was forbidden to the church was not necessarily forbidden to the state. The state was charged with the colony's commission. The state was responsible for suppressing heresy as well as drunkenness and theft and murder. In the hands of the state's government, then, lay the final, supreme responsibility. And John Winthrop came to Massachusetts as the head of that government. He had scarcely arrived when he began a series of moves to make of it a simple but effective instrument for controlling separatism and maintaining a colony united in the execution of God's commission.

VII

A Due Form of Government

When Winthrop and eleven other members of the Massachusetts Bay Company met at Cambridge, England, on August 26, 1629, they agreed to go to New England if the charter and headquarters of the company could be transferred with them. Ten of the twelve kept their pledge, eight of them arriving with Winthrop or shortly after. Besides these, Winthrop could count only four or five other members of the company in New England at the end of 1630. This handful of men was now the Massachusetts Bay Company and endowed with all the powers described in the charter which Winthrop guarded among his papers.

In the charter the King had granted authority "to make, ordeine, and establishe all manner of wholesome and reasonable orders, lawes, statutes, and ordinances, directions, and instructions, not contrarie to the lawes of this our realm of England, as well for setling of the forms and ceremonies of government and magistracy fitt and necessary for the said plantation, and the inhabitants there, and for nameing and stiling of all sortes of officers, both superior and inferior, which they shall finde needeful for that governement and plantation, and the distinguishing and setting forth of the severall duties, powers, and lymytts of every such office and place."

It was intended, of course, that these extensive powers should be exercised by a corporation meeting in England; but the charter did not say so, and the only actual limitation which the King placed on the company's governmental authority over Massachusetts Bay was that it should make no laws repugnant to the laws of England. Settlers going to the colony from England and their children born there were to enjoy "all liberties and immunities" that they would have had if they had been born in England. But English birth did not in 1630 confer the right to participate in government, and the charter did not specify that the consent of the settlers should be obtained for the laws made to govern them. Instead the company had full powers to legislate for the colony and to organize a government to carry out their decrees in any way they saw fit.

With regard to the organization and government of the company itself, the charter was much more specific. The members, known as "freemen," were to meet four times a year in a "Great and General Court," to make laws for both company and colony. Once a year, at one of these courts, they would elect a governor, a deputy governor, and eighteen "assistants" for the coming year, to manage affairs between meetings of the General Court. This executive council was to meet every month. The governor or deputy governor and at least six of the assistants must be present also at every meeting of the General Court, but the charter did not specify that any other members must be present to constitute a quorum, so that these seven officers, in the absence of any other members, could presumably exercise all the powers of the General Court.

In Massachusetts, therefore, Winthrop and the dozen or so members of the company who came with him had unlimited authority to exercise any kind of government they chose over the other settlers. In order to satisfy the terms of the charter they had only to meet once a month as assistants (all but one of the members who are known to have migrated the first year were assistants) and four times a year as a General Court, though the two types of meeting would now be virtually indistinguishable in membership. Provided they followed this procedure and passed no laws repugnant to the laws of England, they could govern Massachusetts in any way they saw fit. And for that matter, who was to say what law was repugnant to those of England? Who was to decide, who to correct them if they erred? Here was no King, Parliament, bishop, or judge to stand in their way.

A group of men as sure of their cause as were Winthrop and his friends must have been strongly tempted to establish themselves as a permanent aristocracy or oligarchy, holding fast the power granted in the charter and using it to enforce the special commission which they believed God had given them. They were a determined, stiff-jawed set, quick to anger and slow to laughter, as likely a group of oligarchs as ever assembled. John Endecott and Thomas Dudley, after Winthrop the most influential of the group, were also the most headstrong.

Endecott had been governing the colony under instructions from the company in England before Winthrop and the others got there. Winthrop saw no need for any such subordinate officer after his own arrival on the scene, but Endecott was still a member of the company and entitled to a place in its councils. He was a soldier by past experience and by temperament, impatient of civilian impertinence, all too ready to draw his sword or strike out with a fist when his commands were not obeyed with alacrity. The General Court commissioned him to keep the peace in Salem, where he continued to live, but his notion of keeping the peace was sometimes far from peaceful. On one occasion, when a man had not treated him with due respect, he felt obliged to defend his dignity with his fists. When Winthrop rebuked him, he answered, "I acknowledge I was too rash in strikeing him, understanding since that it is not lawfull for a justice of peace to strike. But if you had seene the manner of his carriadge, with such daring of mee with his armes on kembow etc. It would have provoked a very patient man." And this John Endecott was not.

Neither was Thomas Dudley, who as deputy governor was Winthrop's second-in-command. Dudley was a rigid, literal-minded type, ready to exact his pound of flesh whenever he thought it due him. As steward of the Earl of Lincoln in England he had prided himself on getting the Earl out of debt by raising the tenants' rents. In Massachusetts he engrossed quantities of corn and lent it to his poorer neighbors on credit, to receive ten bushels for seven and a half after harvest. Winthrop regarded this practice as oppressive usury, but Dudley's temper flared when his conduct was questioned in any way. He was obviously not the sort of man to diminish his own authority.

Winthrop himself was more mature than Dudley or Endecott would ever be. His long struggle with his passions had left him master of himself in a way that few men ever achieve. The fire was still there, and if blown up by other men's wrath, it would occasionally burst out, but generally it lay well below the surface, imparting a warmth and power which everyone around him sensed. Winthrop, as he himself realized, had acquired a talent for command. He never grasped for authority as Dudley or Endecott might, but he did not need to: he was the kind of man upon whom authority was inevitably thrust.

These three men, all disposed in their different ways to command those around them, were equipped also with a philosophy of government to give their commands a superhuman sanction. For more than a hundred years Protestants had been confronting the pope with declarations of the God-given authority of civil rulers. In England Anglican and Puritan alike maintained the divine right of their king against the enemy at Rome, who claimed a power to depose Protestant monarchs. Though the Puritans reserved to the people a right of resistance against tyrants who violated the laws of God, they were always ready to quote the Epistle to the Romans in support of rulers who enforced the laws of God. And the members of the Massachusetts Bay Company were all godly men; they had come with no other intention than to see God's will done at last.

Winthrop never lost an opportunity to affirm his belief that the powers that be were ordained of God and must be honored and respected accordingly. While still aboard the *Arbella,* he had reminded the other passengers that "God Almightie in his most holy and wise providence hath soe disposed of the Condicion of mankinde, as in all times some must be rich some poore, some highe and eminent in power and dignitie; others meane and in subjeccion." There was no doubt in Winthrop's mind that God intended civil governments to be in the hands of men like himself; to entrust the people at large with powers of government, as in a Greek democracy, was not only unwarranted by Scripture but dangerous to the peace and well-being of the community, for the people at large were unfit to rule. The best part of them was always the smallest part, "and of that best part the wiser part is always the lesser."

Winthrop and the other members of the Bay Company were authorized by their charter to exercise absolute powers of government; they were endowed by temperament with the inclination to exercise those powers; and they were assisted by a philosophy of government which clothed every civil ruler in the armor of divine authority. How natural, then, that they should become a ruling oligarchy. They might readily have succumbed to the lust for power, since power lay unchallenged in their hands.

But they did not succumb.

They did not even keep the powers to which the charter entitled them.

After Winthrop had explored the bay and moved the headquarters of the colony from Salem to Charlestown, he summoned the assistants for their first meeting on August 23, 1630. There were seven members present besides himself and Dudley, and they got down to the business of government at once. They provided for the maintenance of two ministers, set maximum wages for workmen in various trades, and appointed a beadle "to attend upon the Governor, and alwaies to be ready to execute his commands in publique businesses." They also ordered that there should be regular meetings, or "courts," of the assistants and of the General Court, though the difference between the two would be a formality, since their membership would be virtually identical (unless future emigration brought over other company members without the status of assistant). On September 7 and September 28 they met again as assistants and exercised their authority in a variety of actions. They forbade the sale of firearms to the Indians; they put an embargo on corn; they seized Richard Clough's strong water because he sold too much of it to other men's servants; and they fined Sir Richard Saltonstall, one of their own number, for being absent from court.

Then on October 19 Winthrop summoned at Charlestown the first meeting labeled in the records as a General Court. For this day he and the seven company members who met with him had prepared a revolution that was to affect the history of Massachusetts from that time forward. The records described the event with tantalizing brevity: "For the establishinge of the government. It was propounded if it were not the best course that the Freemen should have the power of chuseing Assistants when there are to be chosen, and the Assistants from amongst themselves to chuse a Governor and Deputy Governor, whoe with the Assistants should have the power of makeing lawes and chuseing officers to execute the same."

This was surely a strange proposal to make to a group of men all of whom were both freemen and assistants. Why, when there were no freemen but themselves in the colony, should they make provision for freemen electing the assistants and the assistants electing the other officers? One begins to get an inkling of what was happening in the next sentence of the records: "This was fully assented unto by the generall vote of the people, and ereccion of hands."

The "people" here referred to were not simply the eight company members present. This we can conclude from events that followed. Winthrop had apparently thrown open the first meeting of the General Court to the whole body of settlers assembled at Charlestown. Together they had established the first constitution of Massachusetts. It used the terminology of the charter, and presumably allowed the provisions of the charter not expressly revised to remain in effect. But by general vote of the people of Massachusetts, the assistants were transformed from an executive council into a legislative assembly; and the term "freeman" was transformed from a designation for the members of a commercial company, exercising legislative and judicial control over that company and its property, into a designation for the citizens of a state, with the right to vote and hold office. The right of the citizen freemen to vote, however, was confined to electing assistants. These assistants, and not the freemen themselves, were to make laws and appoint from their own number a governor and deputy governor.

This transformation of the Bay Company's charter into a constitution for government of the colony would scarcely have been necessary or desirable if the members of the company had intended to keep control in their own hands. The reduction of the freemen's role in the government and the securing of popular consent to this change presaged the admission to freemanship of a large proportion of settlers, men who could contribute to the joint stock nothing but godliness and good citizenship. The transformation of trading company into commonwealth was completed at the next meeting of the General Court, when one hundred and sixteen persons were admitted as freemen. (This was probably most, if not all, of the adult males, excluding servants, then in the colony.) The new freemen then voted that elections should be annual and, doubtless at the behest of Winthrop, that "for time to come noe man shalbe admitted to the freedome of this body polliticke, but such as are members of some of the churches within the lymitts of the same." Though stated in the form of a limitation, this declaration was in fact an open invitation to every future church member in Massachusetts to take up the privileges of freemanship.

Since the people had no political rights under the charter, Winthrop had given them a role to which they had had no legal claim at all. That he confined the gift to church members was not surprising: he would scarcely have wished to take into partnership all of the multitude of men who might come to his colony for the wrong reasons, and the qualified franchise might also help attract the right kind of settlers. By limiting freemanship to church members he extended political rights to a larger proportion of the people than enjoyed such rights in England—and to people who were better qualified to use them than the mere possessors of a forty-shilling freehold. The question that needs to be answered is not why he limited suffrage but why he extended it. What induced Winthrop and the other members of the Bay Company to resign voluntarily the exclusive powers which the charter conferred on them and which their political beliefs and native dispositions made congenial?

Possibly they gave way to popular demand, but there is no evidence that any such demand existed. Possibly they felt a need to keep their own ranks filled. With sickness and death whittling away at their number, they were already close to the minimum quota of seven assistants required by the charter for the holding of the Assistants Court (only six were required in the General Court). But granting their need to perpetuate themselves, they could still have filled vacancies with a few hand-picked men as the need arose. The charter gave them express permission to admit new members to the company if they chose, but it put them under no obligation to do so. Even a popular demand, if it existed, could have been met by a less drastic measure than the one they took.

The real answer as to why they opened the door to freemanship so wide is to be found in the terms of the commission with which they believed the colony was entrusted. The idea of a "covenant," or contract, between God and man occupied a preeminent place in their thought: it was the basis of an individual's salvation; it was the origin of every true church and also of every state. "It is of the nature and essence of every society," Winthrop once wrote, "to be knitt together by some Covenant, either expressed or implyed." God's special commission to Massachusetts was an implied covenant.

But there was more than one covenant involved in the establishment of any society. After the people joined in covenant with God, agreeing to be bound by His laws, they must establish a government to see those laws enforced, for they did not have enough virtue to carry out their agreement without the compulsive force of government. They must decide among themselves what form of government they wanted and then create it by a voluntary joint compact—a second covenant.

Winthrop evidently thought that the mere act of coming to Massachusetts constituted a sufficient acceptance of the basic covenant, the special commission which God had given the colony. But the second covenant, establishing the government, required a more explicit agreement. Though the King's charter gave the Bay Company a clear and exclusive right to govern the territory, the King's authority was insufficient. The "due form of government" which Winthrop believed the special commission called for could originate only from a covenant between the settlers and the men who were to rule them. Hence the extraordinary action of October 19, with its sequel, the extension of freemanship.

Winthrop did not believe that in extending freemanship he had transformed Massachusetts into a democracy. The legislative power was lodged not in the people but in a select group where, according to his reading of the Bible, it belonged. Nor was Winthrop's action in securing the consent of the people to his government an affirmation of the principle that governments derive their just powers from the consent of the governed. He did not believe that the officers chosen under the new system would be simply the agents of the people who elected them. Rulers, however selected, received their authority from God, not from the people, and were accountable to God, not to the people. Their business was to enforce the nation's covenant with God, and during their term of office, so long as they devoted themselves to this business, they were free to act as they thought best, suiting their actions to the circumstances.

Winthrop did believe that the people, or a properly qualified portion of them, were entitled to determine the form of government to be established over them and to select the persons who should run that government. These two operations performed, their role was played out until, under the form of government they had chosen, it was time to elect new rulers. If a ruler failed in his duty to enforce the laws of God, the people would be obliged to turn him out without waiting for election time. But so long as he did his duty, his authority was absolute, and, regardless of any errors of judgment he might make, the people were obliged to submit. Indeed, anything less than submission would be rebellion against the authority of God.

In Winthrop's view, then, he had not in any way limited or reduced the authority of government by extending to church members a voice in the selection of the men who were to exercise the authority. Rather he had given to government a practical strength which it could not otherwise have possessed, for Winthrop was enough of a politician to know that, regardless of any divine authority a ruler might claim, people would submit to him more readily if they had a voice in choosing him, especially a Puritan people well educated by their ministers in the principle of government based on covenant.

There was a danger, of course, that the people would choose the wrong kind of men to rule them. Government was a difficult business, not something that one honest man could do as well as another. It required not only virtue but learning and wisdom as well: learning because the laws of God were not so obvious that he who runs might read them, wisdom because the ruler must be able to apply the laws every day to new situations and choose the right law for the case in hand. But the limitation of freemanship to church members furnished some insurance against the wiles of demagogues. Winthrop counted on the ministers to give the people sound advice and to instruct them about the kind of men who were best fitted to rule.

The ministers must not seek public office themselves, and there was little likelihood that they would or that they would succeed if they did. Though the ministers enjoyed a powerful influence over their congregations, the shadow of Rome still lay heavily on the Puritans. None of them wanted a "theocracy" in the sense of a government by the clergy. Indeed, of all the governments in the Western world at the time, that of early Massachusetts gave the clergy least authority. As long as Winthrop lived, ministers neither sought nor obtained government office. Their advice was frequently asked and frequently given; their influence over the people was invaluable; but authority rested firmly in the hands of laymen.

Under the new constitution Winthrop and most of the

original assistants were reelected until 1634. With the explicit consent of the new body of freemen and the support of the ministers, they moved swiftly and with assurance to establish in Massachusetts the kind of society that God's commission called for. The offense which they dealt with most severely was contempt of their God-given authority. The New World, with a three-thousand-mile moat on the one hand and boundless free land on the other, offered strong temptation to adventurous spirits to kick over the traces and defy every kind of authority. The American frontiersman with his fine scorn for the restrictions of civilization had not yet emerged, but he had his prototype in men like Maverick and Blackstone, who had thought Massachusetts Bay a good enough place before the saints arrived to purify it. A number of such men were on hand when the Great Migration began, and more came with it. If the Puritan experiment was to succeed, they would have to be kept strictly in check or else removed. Blackstone removed himself to the Narragansett country, remarking that he had left England because he did not like the Lord Bishops and found the rule of the Lord Brethren no better. Maverick remained behind but moved to the comparative isolation of Noddle's Island, where his bibulous hospitality frequently annoyed the government. Others, less discreet than these two, got themselves whipped and fined and banished. John Stone, for example, the captain of a small pinnace, was suspected of adultery, and his vessel was stayed until the matter could be investigated, whereupon he went to Roger Ludlow, one of the justices, and called him "just ass." This kind of punning was dangerous, and though a grand jury could not find enough evidence to indict him for adultery, he was given a suspended fine of a hundred pounds for his contempt of authority and ordered not to enter the colony again without permission on pain of death.

In operating their new government, Winthrop and the

assistants did not differentiate sharply between judicial and legislative functions. Guided by the laws of God as set down in the Bible and fortified with the absolute authority to enforce those laws in any way they saw fit, they felt little need for explicit legislation. They needed no law, for example, to tell them that Mr. Clearke was looking too longingly at the mistress of the family in which he lived, Mrs. Freeman, "concerning whome there is strong suspicion of incontinency"; they simply forbade Mr. Clearke to live with the Freemans or to keep company with Mrs. Freeman. Nor did they need any special law to justify their punishment of Nicholas Knopp by a fine of five pounds "for takeing upon him to cure the scurvey by a water of noe worth nor value, which hee solde att a very deare rate." Since adultery, which was punishable by death under the Biblical code, had seldom been punished in England at all, the court did legislate explicitly on that subject, providing the punishment God demanded. But for the most part their general orders dealt with prudential matters, such as the times for burning land to clear it, the cutting of timber, the fixing of bounties on wolves, the fencing of corn, and the disposal of straying cattle and swine.

Because they were free to act without restraint, by enjoining good actions as well as punishing bad ones they could keep a sharp watch on every kind of heresy and nip ill weeds in the bud. They could argue men out of dangerous positions before an impasse was reached, and doubtless the effectiveness of their arguments owed much to the fact that the authority of the state could enforce them if necessary.

The way Winthrop operated this government and the kind of problems he had to deal with are both well illustrated in a case that arose in 1631 in Watertown, where Winthrop's former neighbor, George Phillips, was pastor. About a year after he and Winthrop arrived together on the *Arbella,* Phillips voiced the opinion that not only the churches of England but those of Rome too were true churches, and he succeeded in convincing many of his congregation. This was separatism inverted: the Reformation had been put through on the assumption that the Catholic Church was incurable, was no true church; it was too late now to give up the Reformation. Winthrop went to Watertown and debated before the congregation against Phillips and Richard Brown, the ruling elder (a lay officer). All but three of the liberals concluded that their opinion was an error.

Richard Brown was one of the three, an intransigent liberal. The Watertown church, probably under Winthrop's influence, formally condemned Brown's too charitable view of Catholicism but did not proceed against him for holding it. He was not even removed from office as ruling elder. The church evidently did not consider this a fatal error, and no doubt Winthrop agreed with them.

A few months later, however, another troublesome party arose in the congregation. Since Elder Brown held an erroneous opinion, some of the members felt they could not pollute themselves by remaining as communicants in the same church with him. This was a more serious matter. Again Winthrop hurried off to Watertown and this time persuaded the purists that they were going too far. There was a general reconciliation; but one John Masters, the leader of the purist faction, apparently had second thoughts afterwards and still refused to take communion with Brown, turning his back whenever the service was performed. Masters, by his exclusiveness, was committing a very serious mistake, for when he steadfastly refused to reform, the church placed its most severe penalty, excommunication, on him, after which he came round and was restored.

This incident epitomized the problem that Winthrop had wrestled with and conquered in his own life and now faced as governor. Because he had learned so painfully and so well that there was no honorable escape from the sins and perils and temptations of the world, he determined from the beginning that New England must not be an escape. The position taken by John Masters pointed straight toward escape. It could lead to the ultimate absurdity of complete withdrawal into oneself, nobody being quite pure enough to join with. It would not only separate New England from the rest of the world but also split it into a host of little communities, each repudiating the others as insufficiently holy.

The position taken by Richard Brown, on the other hand, was equally dangerous to God's commission, for it led to moral indifference, to the obliteration of the distinction between Catholic and Protestant, which for Winthrop was as much as to say the distinction between right and wrong. Neither position could be allowed, but Winthrop sensed that the colony had more to fear from Masters's error than from Brown's. The most dangerous tendency among the saints of Massachusetts was not excessive liberality but excessive purity. In either case the solution lay in early and flexible treatment. Winthrop caught the danger before it got out of hand, and he did not have to prosecute anyone. The members of the church had been reasonable. After he argued them round, they handled the problem themselves.

This was the way to deal with men who wanted to be too good, and the form of government he had established gave him the maximum freedom to deal with them in this way. Absolute authority, resting on a consent that was renewed every year—this was the formula to keep zealots and scamps alike under control.

But the happy combination, happy at least in Winthrop's eyes, was not to last.

VIII

Leniency Rebuked

The great advantage of the government which Winthrop established in Massachusetts was its simplicity. Though it kept contact with the people by annual elections, it was otherwise a despotism with all the efficiency of despotism. It could move with speed when speed was needed and slowly when it was not. It could be lenient or severe as the occasion indicated. No cumbersome political machinery carried the governors helplessly this way or that against their wills, and no complicated body of laws dictated their decisions in every instance.

These advantages counted for much in a new colony in a new world, where preconceived rules would be constantly rubbing against unforeseen difficulties. But despotism, with all its advantages, can never be more efficient or more just or more intelligent than its despots. In the first three elections under the constitution of 1630 the freemen reelected all the men who had held office before. The success of the government thus depended to a large degree on the abilities of Winthrop, Dudley, Endecott, and the original members of the company.

Winthrop was well equipped to exercise the powers he enjoyed. Patient, conscientious, firm but not arbitrary, he was the very soul of discretion. But he had his shortcomings. Surrounded by some of England's most brilliant young theologians, he was not himself a brilliant thinker.

He was prone to take a position, perhaps intuitively, and then support it in lawyerlike fashion by every conceivable argument, even by arguments inconsistent with one another. He could see too easily the hand of God operating in his favor whenever his opponents met with some misfortune, and he took a morbid satisfaction in such events. Though he was not a vindictive man, he was distressingly fond of saying "I told you so" whenever his advice was rejected and things went wrong.

If Winthrop himself had such faults, the magistrates who were elected to serve with him (the deputy governor and the assistants) had others of a kind most unsuitable to anyone entrusted with such extensive powers. To be worthy of their authority they had to know when to be strict and when to be lenient, when to sacrifice purity to charity, when to insist and when to wheedle. They had to know how to be Puritans without being doctrinaire. The two magistrates who still carried the most weight, next to Winthrop, did not know any of these things.

Endecott unfortunately combined a hasty temper with a tendency to carry all beliefs to their logical conclusions or absurdities. In 1633 he happened to be present at a lecture in Boston when the speaker, the Reverend John Cotton, was asked whether women ought to wear veils in church. This was one of those details about which conscientious Puritans were likely to become too concerned. Cotton considered the question and concluded that veils were not necessary. Endecott was on his feet at once to argue that they were. Winthrop records with his usual economy that "after some debate, the governour, perceiving it to grow to some earnestness, interposed, and so it brake off." Endecott was just the man to make an issue out of women's veils, and the following year he all but turned the colony upside down by publicly cutting the cross out of the royal flag.

There was, however, an attractive impetuosity about

Endecott, a warmth that made his shortcomings easy to forgive. Dudley, who occupied a more important position, was a colder man, with a simplicity that was far from attractive. His insistence on the last jot and tittle of the law prevailed not only where he pleaded his own cause, but also in every case that came before him. On one occasion in 1633 Winthrop and the assistants were drafting an answer to an accusation made against them in England by one of the ne'er-do-wells they had shipped back there. Dudley refused to subscribe to the statement, because, in repeating the words of the accusation, the statement referred to the bishops as "reverend bishops" and also designated the King as his "sacred majesty" and professed a common belief in Christianity with the churches of England. Thomas Dudley had subscribed the Humble Request aboard the *Arbella,* but the New World was affecting him as it affected others: he now thought it would pollute him to recognize the Anglican Church.

This was precisely the kind of belligerent precisionism that Winthrop hoped to overcome by keeping the government unencumbered with rules and formalities. But how could he overcome separatism when the government itself had become infested with it? As might be expected, Winthrop's relations with Dudley were none too happy, and Dudley, more than any other single individual, frustrated the scheme of government which Winthrop had inaugurated in the meeting of October 1630.

Part of the trouble was personal, and Winthrop may have been as much at fault as Dudley. During the early part of the first winter in New England the assistants had decided to build their houses at Cambridge (then called Newtown) and make that the capital of the colony. Accordingly Winthrop and Dudley began construction. But it became obvious as the months passed that Boston made a more convenient site than Cambridge. Winthrop seems never to have occupied his house and eventually took it down. Perhaps Dudley could not afford to do the same or to build a second house. In any case he stayed in Cambridge and felt that Winthrop treated him badly by not becoming his neighbor. Nor did Winthrop improve matters any when he told Dudley "that he did not well to bestow such cost about wainscotting and adorning his house, in the beginning of a plantation."

The difficulty between the two men was more than personal. Dudley not only lacked the discretion that Winthrop thought important in a magistrate; he disagreed that discretion was important or desirable. Dudley, as deputy governor, was close enough to the throne to be piqued at not occupying it; and the fact that he had been maneuvered into a settlement away from the center of things probably made him particularly sensitive to anything that looked like a neglect of his own office. Winthrop, it seemed to him, was exceeding his authority by taking independent action in matters that were the business of the Assistants Court.

The manner of Winthrop's defection, in Dudley's eyes, lay in being not severe enough. He was too easy on offenders, too lenient, failing to have punishments fully executed, failing to levy fines as strictly as he should. When men were banished from the colony by order of the court, he had allowed them to linger on for weeks at a time before finally expelling them. He had lent twenty-eight pounds of gunpowder to Plymouth colony without authorization. He had constructed a fort at Boston. He had let the people of Watertown build a weir on the Charles River. All these actions Dudley interpreted as a bid for popularity. Winthrop, he thought, was playing the demagogue and extending his own power at the expense of the deputy governor and assistants.

Dudley made his charges honestly to Winthrop's face at a meeting where several ministers were present; and Winthrop answered them all. The fort had been agreed upon a year before, and he had built it at his own expense. The gunpowder he had lent to Plymouth was his own, and badly needed. He had given the permission to Watertown because its people were low on provisions. If they had waited to ask permission of the court, the fishing season would have been past, "and, for his part, he would employ all his power in the court, so as he should sink under it, if it were not allowed." As for the men banished, he had power as governor to stay execution until the next meeting of the court, and he had done it because their sentence was delivered in winter: execution at once would have endangered their lives. Levying fines, he said, was the secretary's business, not his, "yet he confessed, that it was his judgment, that it were not fit, in the infancy of a commonwealth, to be too strict in levying fines, though severe in other punishments." Winthrop later admitted a general belief "that in the infancy of plantations, justice should be administered with more lenity than in a settled state, because people were then more apt to transgress, partly of ignorance of new laws and orders, partly through oppression of business and other straits."

This was a dangerous admission in a colony where the freemen were bent on observing their covenant with God. Dudley's preference for executing the laws of God with unbending rigor struck a responsive chord among the pious men and women who had seen too much lenity at home in England. Lenity meant cockfights and theaters and sports on Sunday. Lenity meant lofty prelates unrebuked by the government. Lenity meant ceremonies and rituals unwarranted by God's word. To Winthrop, of course, it meant none of these things. Yet there was a real issue here, the old issue of uncompromising purity versus charity. Winthrop, on the side of charity, sought the true course in judicial discretion rather than legislative precision.

At the same meeting where he exposed Winthrop's leniency, Dudley also attacked Winthrop on another front.

At the outset he demanded to know whether Winthrop claimed authority by the charter or otherwise. By Winthrop's standards this was a blow below the belt. If he claimed authority by virtue of the constitutional agreement of the people, of October 1630, rather than by the charter, the word would quickly go round that Massachusetts was setting up as an independent state. Such an answer would have invited trouble from England, as Dudley well knew. Winthrop dodged the question by asserting that he "would challenge no greater authority than he might by the patent." Dudley replied "that then he had no more authority than every assistant (except power to call courts, and precedency, for honor and order)." Winthrop replied that since the charter called him a governor he had whatever power belonged to a governor by common law. Angry at being forced into this position, he spoke, as he put it, "somewhat apprehensively," so that "the deputy [i.e., Deputy Governor Dudley] began to be in passion, and told the governour, that if he were so round, he would be round too. The governour bad him be round, if he would. So the deputy rose up in great fury and passion, and the governour grew very hot also, so as they both fell into bitterness."

This scene occurred on a summer's afternoon in 1632, and Winthrop's administration survived it for nearly two more years. But word of the meeting inevitably circulated, for Dudley had given the freemen a great deal to think about. Besides calling attention to Winthrop's leniency, which worried the most zealous of them, he had raised a question in their minds about the governor's authority, and they were already uneasy about the discretion Winthrop claimed and practiced. Though they could freely acknowledge that the authority of rulers came from God, Englishmen had long ago learned to fear a government that had no specific laws to restrain it. Winthrop might assure them that the Scriptures were a sufficient map to steer by, but they felt that the course should be charted and the shoals marked. And what was more, they wanted to have a hand in marking them.

The first sign that they were not altogether pleased with Winthrop's government came very early, before Dudley had made his complaint against leniency. It came from Watertown, where Pastor Phillips and Elder Brown had already brewed Winthrop one batch of trouble. He had scarcely talked the people there out of their misguided acknowledgment of Rome, when he heard that they had fallen into a more dangerous error. The government having levied a tax to build fortifications at Newtown (Cambridge), Phillips and Brown persuaded the people not to pay it, "for fear of bringing themselves and posterity into bondage."

Phillips and Brown were affirming the principle for which Winthrop's friends Sir Nathaniel Barnardiston and Sir Francis Barrington had already suffered imprisonment in England, the principle which Americans would one day follow to independence, that no taxes may be levied on a man without his consent, given in person or by his representatives. But was the principle being violated? Winthrop thought not, and the wisdom of his extension of freemanship now became apparent. Without it he would have had to tell the rebels that the charter gave absolute powers to the company, an answer that would have confirmed their fears. Instead when he summoned them before the Court of Assistants, he was able to point out, though no general election had yet taken place (only nine months had elapsed since the first new freemen were sworn in), that they had nothing to fear from a government which they themselves were entitled to elect, whereupon "they acknowledged their fault, confessing freely, that they were in an error, and made a retraction and submission under their hands."

The error of the Watertowners, Winthrop pointed out,

was "that they took this government to be no other but as of a mayor and aldermen, who have not power to make laws or raise taxations without the people." If Phillips and Brown thought that the government of Massachusetts was merely that of an English borough, they did well to protest, for the mayor and aldermen who governed most English boroughs were self-perpetuating corporations, in which the people ordinarily had no share. Aldermen were elected by other aldermen whenever a death occurred in their own ranks. They also chose the mayor, usually for a one-year term, but they themselves held office for life. These petty oligarchies did not usually have the power to tax, but otherwise they enjoyed an almost absolute power within their boroughs.

The government of a borough, in other words, was very much like that which the Massachusetts Bay Company could have exercised over Massachusetts, except that the company's powers were even more extensive than those of most borough corporations. Winthrop was not using sophistry when he told the people of Watertown that the government of Massachusetts was not (he might have said "no longer") like this, that it was "rather in the nature of a parliament, and that no assistant could be chosen but by the freemen, who had power likewise to remove the assistants and put in others, and therefore at every general court (which was to be held once every year) they had free liberty to consider and propound anything concerning the same, and to declare their grievances, without being subject to question." Winthrop said, in other words, that the assistants were, like Parliament, representatives of the people, an elected body with supreme legislative and judicial authority. They were, to be sure, a small parliament, but the colony itself was small, and the ratio of representatives to population was actually a good deal larger than it was in the House of Commons.

What Winthrop failed to take into account, however,

was that every assistant in Massachusetts was to be elected at large, by all the voters, not just by those of a particular locality. In England most members of the House of Commons were elected locally on local issues and served local interests while they sat in Parliament. The settlers of Massachusetts, like the Englishmen they left behind, thought of a representative, when they thought of him at all, as someone who would promote the special interests of his borough or county, someone who would know what taxes his constituents could bear and what they could not, how they would be affected by passage of this bill or by failure to pass that one. Winthrop's own earlier experience in Suffolk County elections should have made him aware of the value to government of men with knowledge of local conditions and needs.

Whether or not the Watertowners reminded him of this is not recorded, but ten weeks later when election time came round, the General Court ordered that two men be chosen from every plantation to confer with the governor and assistants about raising taxes. Winthrop explained why: "So as what they should agree upon should bind all." This was precisely the kind of measure he approved. Provided the representatives so chosen confined themselves to the matter of taxes, they would not interfere with the efficiency of the government, and their presence would forestall discontent.

Winthrop also agreed to another innovation at the same meeting of the General Court in 1632, namely that the election of governor and deputy governor be transferred from the assistants to the freemen. Winthrop knew in advance that the freemen were going to propose this measure and urged the assistants to accept it. Some of them were much put out. One in particular, Roger Ludlow, who later became a leading figure in Connecticut, "grew into passion and said, that then we should have no government, but there would be an interim, wherein every man might do what he pleased." Winthrop was able to reassure the rest of the assistants that the measure would bring no such disastrous consequence, but Ludlow "continued stiff in his opinion, and protested he would then return back into England." The measure passed; Ludlow remained; and the freemen reelected Winthrop just as the assistants would have done.

Still the uneasiness about the government persisted, fed by Dudley's charges against the governor's leniency and Winthrop's admission that the authority of the government rested on the charter. Sooner or later someone would think to ask what the charter actually had to say about it. And then, inevitably, the freemen of the colony would claim as their own right all the powers that were conferred by the charter on the freemen of the original company. The word "freemen" as used in Massachusetts after 1630 meant something more and something less than was intended in the charter. The charter had used the word to designate the stockholders of the company, a body not too numerous to act as a legislative assembly. Before Winthrop extended the term to mean citizens of the colony, the settlers had consented that the term should no longer include any legislative power. If freemanship had been extended to all church members without this rule, the effect would have been to make Massachusetts a simple democracy, with hundreds of citizens gathering in some huge field to make laws. Winthrop and the other members of the company would doubtless have preferred to keep all powers in their own hands rather than establish a government of that kind. Nevertheless, since freemanship had been extended and Dudley had forced Winthrop to acknowledge the charter as the basis of government, the freemen needed only to inspect the document in order to discover that by their title they might claim a direct share in all legislation. They would certainly be disposed to make the claim, feeling as they did that legislation was needed to limit the discretion of their rulers.

The matter came to a head in the spring of 1634, when notices went out for the annual court of election to be held in May. The freemen chose a group of two men from each town to plan an agenda of other matters to be considered at this court. When these representatives met, they asked Winthrop for the charter (or "patent," as they generally called it). Upon seeing that it empowered the freemen to make laws, they asked for an explanation.

Winthrop told them that when the patent was granted, the number of freemen was small enough so that all could join in making laws. With the removal to Massachusetts and the opening of freemanship to all church members, the number became so large that it had been necessary to choose a smaller group for that purpose (he meant the assistants, who now performed all legislative, judicial, and executive functions). Perhaps in the future an additional "select company" of freemen might be designated as legislators, but the colony did not at present have "a sufficient number of men qualified for such a business." Nor could it stand the "loss of time" of so many additional men diverted from work to government. Nevertheless, he was willing to have them make a beginning at the coming General Court: they might order that once a year a certain number "be appointed (upon summons from the governour) to revise all laws, etc., and to reform what they found amiss therein; but not to make any new laws, but prefer their grievances to the court of assistants." No taxes would be levied nor any public lands disposed of without consent of this committee.

Winthrop's concessions were real, but they came too late. They still left the governor and assistants a wide discretion beyond the control of the freemen. What the freemen wanted was a full body of legislation, made by themselves or their representatives, as a guarantee against arbitrary government. Though the constitution of 1630 allowed them to elect their despots every year, they retained a healthy aversion to despotism as such, elective or hereditary, benevolent or otherwise. It was Winthrop's greatest weakness that he failed to see the merit of their view. He never ceased to think that government should be as little confined by legislation as possible.

If he had held this opinion with the same doctrinaire fervor that Endecott and Dudley displayed in less important matters, he might have lost his influence in the colony very quickly. Fortunately Winthrop's commanding position did not depend on abstract theories or legal documents. The same sense for political realities that enabled him to bring the church members into partnership in the Bay Company also enabled him to give way gracefully before popular demands when it seemed imperative to do so.

He gave way now as the freemen, following Dudley's lead, insisted on the patent as the constitution of the colony. When they met for election, they ordered that the four yearly General Courts should be held as prescribed by the patent. Realizing, however, that it would be impossible for such a large body to operate effectively, they provided that the freemen should be present only at the court for elections and at the others should send deputies from every town to act in their place, thus establishing a government in which each community had its own representatives. Winthrop was rebuked by being reduced to the rank of assistant. In his place as governor they chose Thomas Dudley, with Roger Ludlow as deputy governor, him of the hot temper who had threatened to return to England if the freemen were allowed to choose the governor and deputy governor. It is not recorded that he objected to taking office.

Winthrop accepted the change calmly; by his own political philosophy the people were entitled to determine the form of their civil government. Neither in his journal nor in his private letters did he reveal any sense of bitterness or complain of ingratitude. When the General Court demanded an account of the public expenditures during his term of office, he heaped coals of fire upon them by showing that he had frequently dipped into his own pocket to pay the bills of Massachusetts. During the next three years, while other men sat in the governor's chair, he never sulked in his tent but accepted willingly whatever small tasks were assigned him.

Winthrop was still an assistant and consequently a regular member of the General Court and the Assistants Court. In addition, people continued to come to him about matters that the new governor should have handled. Winthrop attributed this to the fact that Dudley lived in Cambridge, while his own house was conveniently located in Boston, but it was more than that. He was still John Winthrop, and his authority did not depend wholly upon votes. People might put other men in office above him, but they could never ignore the authority that Winthrop carried within him. Whoever was governor, he would still be one who governed.

IX

Separatism Unleashed

As long as Winthrop held the reins of government he held them lightly. Though he never hesitated to strike down sin, he was keenly aware that Massachusetts was endangered more by separatist zeal than by worldly wickedness. He knew too that the time to check separatism was early, before it became blind to every obstacle. Argument, admonition, and patience were the most effective weapons against it. Winthrop used them to such advantage that for four years, while the settlers established themselves and their churches, Massachusetts was troubled by no deep rifts between man and man.

After the freemen turned Winthrop out of the governor's chair, they filled it for the three succeeding years with men of a less flexible nature. Thomas Dudley, John Haynes, and Henry Vane were all of a kind, easily intoxicated with their own righteousness. Of John Haynes, who succeeded Dudley as governor in 1635, it is enough to say that he had joined the attack on Winthrop's leniency. Henry Vane, a more complex character, was a mere boy of twenty-three when elected to the governorship in 1636, less than a year after his arrival in Massachusetts. His father was comptroller of the King's household, and he himself had an illustrious career in England ahead of him. At this time he was full of the magnetism, the enthusiasm, and the dedication of youth. Though he had a generosity of nature that was wholly lacking in Dudley, he had the same uncompromising devotion to principle, a devotion that would bring him one day to the scaffold. He was a good man, but a dangerous one to govern a colony already overloaded with zeal.

Though Winthrop's moderation had brought the colony successfully through the crucial first years, separatism still posed a threat to its mission if not to its survival. If the rigidity of his successors should prevail, there would be great danger of crippling schisms and secessions. The Great Migration was filling Massachusetts with men and women who were not afraid to take sides and not afraid to stand up against government. Among them, as it happened, was a man named Roger Williams, a charming, sweet-tempered, winning man, courageous, selfless, God-intoxicated—and stubborn—the very soul of separatism.

Williams had been in on the Massachusetts Bay project as early as Winthrop. During the meeting at Tattershall in 1629, when Winthrop talked the whole thing out with Isaac Johnson and the others, Williams had appeared and had probably taken part in the discussions. He was a young man, fresh from Cambridge, where he had studied divinity. In 1629 he was chaplain to Sir William Masham of High Laver in Essex. Sir William was one of Winthrop's clients in the Court of Wards, and Winthrop had doubtless heard good things of Williams from him.

Williams did not depart with Winthrop and the others in the spring of 1630 but arrived the following February, in the midst of that first dreadful winter. The ship which brought him was the *Lyon*, which Winthrop had sent back for provisions the previous fall. Winthrop noted her cargo approvingly, not only the supply of lemon juice which put an end to scurvy, but also the "godly minister." He arrived at an opportune time, for the Reverend John Wilson, teacher of the Boston church, was returning to England on the *Lyon* to fetch his wife. The congregation invited

Williams to officiate during his absence, and here the first premonition of trouble appeared: he refused the offer. Williams had left England with none of the reluctance that troubled Winthrop and his friends, for Williams was an avowed Separatist: he felt no attachment whatever to the Church of England. In fact, since the churches of England were contaminated by the admission of unregenerate persons to communion, he could not regard them as churches at all. He had befouled himself by attending them in England; now that he was clear of them he cheerfully renounced them and repented his former weakness.

The Boston church, of course, did not admit unregenerate members. It was a true congregational church, open only to those who could prove themselves holy. But this was not enough for Williams. He could not bring himself to soil his new purity by joining in worship with people who, though pure themselves, failed to renounce the impurities of England. "I durst not," he later explained, "officiate to an unseparated people, as upon examination and conference I found them to be." Unless the members of the church would "make a public declaration of their repentance for having communion with the churches of England, while they lived there," he could not accept their offer.

Here was a Separatist indeed, who would separate not only from erroneous churches but also from everyone who would not denounce erroneous churches as confidently as he did. It is not clear whether the Boston church was tempted to accept his demands, but Winthrop assuredly was not. He liked Williams, as most people did, but this sweeping repudiation of the world went against his most deeply felt convictions. He prepared a little argument to demonstrate the necessity of reforming corruption "without an absolute separation." In it he rebuked all Separatists for their self-righteous denunciation of English church members as whores and drunkards. Although most

Englishmen might be ignorant and misguided, he admitted, "yet whores and drunkards they are not: weake
Christians they are indeed, and the weaker for want of
that tender Care, that should be had of them: 1: by those
that are sett over them to feede them: and next for that
spirituall pride, that Sathan rooted into the hearts of their
brethren, who when they are Converted, doe not, nor will
not strengthen them, but doe Censure them, to be none of
Gods people, nor any visible Christians."

Thus Winthrop reproached his young friend. Though
Williams's opinions horrified him, it was characteristic of
Winthrop to meet them with arguments and not merely
with authority. There is no record that he made use of his
position as governor to prevent the Boston church from
accepting Williams's terms, but he may have hinted that
he would do so if necessary, for before leaving Boston
(within a few weeks), Williams expressed the dangerous
opinion that civil magistrates had no authority in any religious matter, that they could not even require people to
keep the Sabbath.

When Williams found that the Boston church was not
pure enough for him, he made his way to Salem, where
once again his charm and earnestness found an immediate
response. In spite of his extreme views he never antagonized people by sanctimoniousness. He had a sweetness of
spirit that clothed his harshest opinions with a mantle of
holiness. He was a palpable saint, and in a society that set
so high a value on sainthood, he could not fail to find men
and women to follow wherever he might lead. At Salem
John Endecott, whose heart was not easily won, capitu-
lated at once. The church made Williams the same offer
that the Boston church had.

Winthrop, hearing of what had happened, was
alarmed, and after conferring with the assistants wrote
sharply to Endecott, "marvelling" that the Salem church
would choose a teacher who held such dangerous views.

Williams's charms had not yet secured a strong enough hold on Salem to withstand the disapproval of the man who had pulled the colony through the starving months just finished, and who held, besides, the authority which God gave to righteous rulers. The offer was withdrawn, and Williams departed for the Plymouth colony, where Separatists were more welcome.

At Plymouth Williams was satisfied for a time. Though he worked hard at the hoe for his bread, as he later re-called, he found the church properly separated from the English churches and was content to join it and to assist the pastor by occasional preaching. William Bradford, the judicious governor of the colony, found him "a man godly and zealous, having many precious parts, but very unset-tled in judgmente." Bradford was writing after the event, and his own judgment may have been unsettled by later developments, but it seems apparent that Williams's meticulous separatism proved too much even for Ply-mouth. In 1633, Bradford noted he "begane to fall into some strang opinions, and from opinion to practise; which caused some controversie betweene the church and him, and in the end some discontente on his parte, by occasion wherof he left them some thing abruptly."

The cause of Williams's discontent, by his own account, was the fact that the Plymouth church had not proved as separatist as he first supposed it to be. When members of the church returned on visits to England, they attended Church of England services there, and were not cast out of the Plymouth church for doing so. In this way the Ply-mouth church was communicating with the churches of England and by implication acknowledging them to be true churches. Williams, by remaining a member, shared in this acknowledgment; therefore he must leave them.

According to Cotton Mather, who wrote two genera-tions later and is not to be taken at face value, Williams was the cause of another controversy at Plymouth. He was troubled, it seems, by the application of the title "Goodman" to unregenerate persons. This term was customarily attached to the names of yeomen, who were not entitled to be called "Master" (the designation of a gentleman) but were a step above common laborers, who bore no title to their names at all. Williams contended that "Goodman" should be reserved for regenerate persons who were truly "good." This was another of those problems that zealous Puritans could become absurdly concerned about, and when Winthrop visited the colony, they put the question to him. He was able to argue away their concern, and so "put a stop to the little, idle, whimsical conceits, then beginning to grow obstreperous." Although Mather's bias is evident, the position attributed to Williams was characteristic of the man: he could follow a belief to its conclusion with a passionate literalness that bordered on the ridiculous.

When he left Plymouth, in 1633, Williams carried his zeal once more to Salem, where his memory was still green. Winthrop had remained his friend, as a letter written by Williams from Plymouth attested, but one may doubt that Winthrop was as happy as the people of Salem were to see the young man back in Massachusetts Bay. At Salem they welcomed him to church membership and cautiously made him an unofficial assistant to the pastor. By not electing him to any church office they probably thought to avoid more trouble with the government. Although the Salem church made no formal renunciation of the English churches, Williams found the members sufficiently sympathetic to his views and almost at once began to lure them along the paths of perfectionism.

While at Plymouth, Williams had raised the question whether the colonists had any right to the land they occupied. Winthrop, hearing of this, now inquired of him about it, and Williams replied with a copy of an argument he had prepared on the subject. In order to appreciate the shock which this document must have given the magistrates of Massachusetts, one must remember that the English Civil War had not begun and that the Massachusetts Bay Company had gained its control over the colony by virtue of a patent from the King. Roger Williams declared that the King's authority to grant such control rested on "a solemn public lie." He also charged the King with blasphemy for referring to Europe as Christendom and applied to the King certain uncomplimentary passages from the Book of Revelation.

The magistrates were horrified by this lese majesty and ordered Williams to appear at the next General Court to be censured. Winthrop, as shocked as the others, took steps at once to see that the confrontation between Williams and the court should not become the occasion for mutual recriminations. He wrote to Endecott, acquainting him with the summons and describing the charges which would be laid against Williams. At the same time he outlined arguments that Endecott could use in bringing Williams to reconsider and retract his offensive views: the King's claim to Massachusetts was founded on no lie, "for his people were the first, that discovered these parts: but admitt he had been mistaken: was it ever knowne, that a true Christian did give his naturall Prince the lye? was he not the Lords annointed?" This and many other arguments Winthrop adduced, some based on Scripture, some based on common sense, and some on nonsense. "If we had no right to this lande," he concluded, "yet our God hathe right to it, and if he be pleased to give it us (taking it from a people who had so longe usurped upon him, and abused his creatures) who shall controll him or his termes?"

Williams was at least sufficiently chastened to appear penitently at the court, "and gave satisfaction," Winthrop records, "of his intention and loyalty. So it was left, and nothing done in it." This was Winthrop's way of dealing with Separatists, and hitherto it had worked. Perhaps even in the talented hands of Winthrop it could not have gone on working with so irrepressible a man as Williams. Perhaps the coming showdown was inevitable. But when it came, Massachusetts was in the hands of men far less able than Winthrop and fortunate indeed to have Winthrop's precedents to follow.

In November 1634, six months after the election of Dudley, the General Court heard that Williams was publicly teaching again that the King's patent was invalid before God and that the churches of England were anti-Christian. Once again the court gave orders for his appearance. Meanwhile, Williams went on arguing with all and sundry to the effect that Massachusetts ought to send the patent back to the King, with a request that he modify it by omitting all clauses relating to donation of land. Unless this were done, the sin of accepting the land from this public liar could not be expiated except by dissolving the colony and returning all the settlers to England, where they could make public acknowledgment of the evil they had done by coming to New England on such false pretenses.

Both alternatives were ridiculous. To insult the King by telling him to rewrite the patent and leave out the lies was as fantastic as to pull up stakes and go home in order to call him a liar at closer range. When the General Court met again in March 1635, Dudley was ready to deal with this madman, but John Cotton, in the name of the other ministers, presented a request that they be given a chance to persuade him privately of his errors. It was a reasonable request, for under Winthrop's rule they had often been consulted before the government took action on religious questions. Dudley, however, replied "that wee were deceived in him [Williams], if we thought he would condescend to learne of any of us: And what will you doe," he asked, "when you have run your course, and found all your labour lost?" Perhaps Dudley could have persuaded the Court of Assistants to let him handle Williams, but owing to his own machinations, the power of government no longer rested in the assistants alone but in the General Court of assistants and deputies. The deputies approved of the precedent set by Winthrop and, in spite of Dudley's opposition, decided to give the ministers a chance to reclaim their brother. The ministers' arguments and perhaps other "Councells from Flesh and Bloud" (as Williams later called them) induced him to abandon his attack on the charter and not to send a letter he had been preparing for the King advising His Majesty that he had been guilty of a lie.

This was the last time Williams troubled the colony about the patent, but at the next meeting of the assistants in April 1635, he was summoned again on another score. About a year before, the magistrates had ordered that all inhabitants who were not freemen should take a resident's oath to support the colony and its government against all enemies. Roger Williams saw in this measure another source of contamination for the godly and proceeded again to sound the alarm. The difficulty lay in the fact that an oath was considered an act of worship. If a magistrate (presumably regenerate) should tender an oath to a non-freeman (presumably unregenerate), he would "thereby have communion with a wicked man in the worship of God, and cause him to take the name of God in vain." Here was Williams's separatism cropping out in still another form. He persuaded Endecott and many others to adopt his view, and though Endecott was quickly argued out of his error, so many people were convinced the government was violating rather than upholding the word of God that the court felt obliged temporarily to drop the oath and with it the charges against Williams.

Williams's separatism now began to spin faster, and he threw off a succession of strange opinions: that a regenerate man ought not to pray in company with an unregenerate one, not even with his wife or children, and that he ought not to give thanks after the sacrament or after meals. He also resumed the dangerous contention which he had first voiced when leaving Boston in 1631, that the civil government had no authority in religious matters, that it could not punish breaches of the first table (the first four of the Ten Commandments) except insofar as such breaches caused a disturbance of civil peace.

Somehow, too, he had been able to set the people of Salem spinning with him. Indeed they were all but bewitched with his heedless holiness, and when their minister, Samuel Skelton, died, they cast off caution and in the spring of 1635 chose Williams in his place—knowing well that the government would quickly move against them.

At the next General Court in July Williams was summoned again, to answer for his growing list of erroneous opinions; and the other ministers were asked to be there too and advise the court what to do with him. As the court met, he was at the height of his furious and indefatigable righteousness and fortified by the fact that as minister of the Salem church he could now claim the acknowledged principle of congregational independence in his defense. Any attempt by other ministers to remove him from office would infringe upon the independence of the Salem church. And any attempt by the government to remove him would be met by a defiant congregation. The ministers consulted and unanimously declared their opinion that any minister who obstinately maintained such opinions as Williams avowed, "whereby a church might run into heresy, apostacy, or tyranny," should be removed, "and that the other churches ought to request the magistrates so to do." The churches might be powerless by the principle of congregational independence, but the civil government was not and prepared at once to carry out the advice of the clergy.

Salem was petitioning the General Court at this time for land in Marblehead Neck; and the General Court, ready to fight with foul means as well as fair, refused the petition unless the Salem church dismissed Williams. The outraged church immediately sent off letters to the other churches urging the members to reprimand the magistrates and the deputies alike for this "heinous sin" (which indeed it was).

In this moment of crisis the future of Williams, of Salem, and of the colony hung precariously in balance. To crush the rebellion of an entire church would have proved a difficult, if not a bloody, if not an impossible, business. To crush it in the face of any widespread sympathy would certainly have split the colony, and had the Salem appeal reached the other churches, the members might have found much in it to win their sympathy.

At this juncture the ministers evidently felt as the General Court did, that any means were justified to keep the colony and its holy commission intact. It was the ministers who received the letters addressed by Salem to the other churches, and they simply refrained from communicating them to their members. But it was Williams himself who broke the deadlock and unwittingly pulled the colony out of danger by a final extravagant gesture, a gesture which proved too much for his Salem admirers. The churches of Massachusetts, he said, had given up the principle of congregational independence and had called in the government to help suppress it. They were no longer pure churches. His congregation must therefore renounce the other churches of Massachusetts. Unless they did so, he would be obliged himself to withdraw from the Salem church.

It was unfortunate for Williams that during this crisis he was confined to his bed by an illness and so forced to resort to letters. When he could support his arguments with his winning personality, they were much more compelling than they could be in writing. Reduced to ink and paper, they were apt to appear tedious, far-fetched, sanctimonious. But even his magnetic personal charm might have been insufficient to bring the people of Salem to the step he now demanded of them. The men and women who read his letter were acutely aware that the rest of the colony was against them, that the authority of government was against them, that the wisdom of other godly ministers was against them. His letter asked them in effect to renounce all the rest of the world, for if there were no true churches in the rest of Massachusetts, where else could there be any?

Winthrop says the whole Salem church was "grieved" with Williams's request. The supreme assurance of a Roger Williams is rare at any time, and in Salem a majority were unwilling to go as far as he asked. Probably some made their decision with one eye on the land of Marblehead Neck. But it is not necessary to assume such weakness for their actions. It is more likely that the majority simply could not bring themselves to declare that everyone outside Salem was wrong.

The final confrontation between Williams and the General Court came early in October 1635 at a full meeting, with all the ministers of the colony invited to attend. The charges preferred against him were of two kinds: his new and dangerous opinions, in particular his denial of the magistrates' authority in religious matters, and his seditious letters, one in the name of the Salem church attacking the General Court, and the second to the Salem church urging their separation from the other churches of the colony.

Williams made no attempt to deny the charges. He was as adamant as Luther at the Diet of Worms, and though offered a month's respite in which to prepare his defense, he waived the offer and justified every opinion. Even Thomas Hooker, the most eloquent spokesman of New England orthodoxy, could not move him. The court therefore ordered him to leave the colony within six weeks.

Returning to Salem (the court was held in Boston), Williams found his church unwilling to support him. His hard core of devoted followers did not constitute a majority. Rather than remain connected with a church which recognized the other churches of Massachusetts, he resigned his office and his membership. Perhaps because he seemed thus to have drawn his own fangs, the General Court extended the date for his departure until the following spring, on condition that he not "go about to draw others to his opinions."

It was a foolish requirement. The court should have known that Williams's charm drew people like a magnet and that he was not the kind of man to be silent simply because his opinions had displeased the government. Before the winter was far gone, the magistrates heard that "he had drawn above twenty persons to his opinion, and they were intended to erect a plantation about the Narragansett Bay, from whence the infection would easily spread into these churches, (the people being, many of them, much taken with the apprehension of his godliness)." The court decided to forestall this move by shipping him back to England. But before they could lay hands on him he was gone, off for Narragansett Bay in a bitter January.

Winthrop recorded the event in his journal without comment. He held Williams's views in the utmost abhorrence, and must have concurred in the sentence of banishment. By the time the sentence was delivered there was no alternative. The people of Massachusetts could scarcely have carried out their commission and allowed Williams to remain.

That Winthrop disapproved, either openly or privately, the move to ship Williams back to England was not suggested by his journal, but it was plainly implied by Williams himself in a letter written many years later. In 1670, when Winthrop was long in his grave, Williams wrote to a friend, "When I was unkindly and unchristianly, as I believe, driven from my house and land and wife and children, (in the midst of a New England winter, now about thirty-five years past,) at Salem, that ever honored Governor, Mr. Winthrop, privately wrote to me to steer my course to Narragansett Bay and Indians, for many high and heavenly and public ends, encouraging me, from the freeness of the place from any English claims or patents. I took his prudent motion as a hint and voice from God, and waving all other thoughts and motions, I steered my course from Salem (though in winter snow, which I feel yet) unto these parts..." Winthrop, unlike the other magistrates of Massachusetts, retained Williams's affection and respect. Indeed, during the first five years of his exile Williams's letters to Winthrop expressed an admiration bordering on adulation.

One of the first of these, written from Providence on October 24, 1636, answered a set of queries evidently sent by Winthrop. Now that the damage was done, Winthrop had asked his friend to cast up accounts: What had he gained by his "new-found practices"? Did he find his spirit as even as it was seven years before, when he and Winthrop first met? Was he not himself grieved to have grieved so many? Did he really think the rest of New England utterly forsaken of God? Could he not have remained in the New England churches without endangering his soul? What, after all, was he aiming at?

Williams's answers were like the man, humble and loving and respectful, but at the same time defiant, with a holy intransigeance. They breathed throughout the spirit of separatism. He did indeed think that the Lord had forsaken New England for failing to separate her churches wholly from the filthiness of English corruption. And to Winthrop he offered the very advice that Winthrop could least willingly listen to. Where Winthrop had urged him to pause and consider whether everyone was wrong but him, he replied with an invitation to join him in splendid isolation: "Abstract yourselfe," he urged, "with a holy violence from the Dung heape of this Earth." Williams would not learn the lesson which Winthrop had taught himself so painfully before he left England, that there was no escape from the dung heap of this earth; and that those who sought one or thought they had found it acted with an unholy, not a holy, violence.

Winthrop watched the subsequent development of Williams's views along a course he might have predicted. Within a year or two Williams decided that the church must not include children simply on the basis of their parents' membership and abandoned the practice of infant baptism in the congregation he had gathered among the handful of the faithful who followed him to Providence. He had himself and all the other members rebaptized, but shortly began to question whether there could be a proper church at all until God raised up some new apostolic power. Finally he reached the position where he could not conscientiously have communion with anyone but his wife.

This was the limit of his separatism. He did not reach the ultimate absurdity of finding no one but himself fit to communicate with. Indeed, from this point forward his separatism, having reached the pinnacle of isolation, broke through to a new realm of freedom, unknown and undesired by other Puritans. While still in Massachusetts he had denied that the state had anything to do with religion, thus making of it an association for purely temporal, worldly purposes. And he had espoused a congregational independence so complete that when put into practice, it necessitated a hitherto unheard-of religious freedom. It must have been painful for a man who set so high a value on purity in religion to stand sponsor at Narragansett for religious opinions that he abhorred. Williams ended the pain by deciding that no church could attain purity in this world. He had effectively demonstrated the proposition to himself as he withdrew successively from the Church of England, from the churches of Massachusetts, and finally from everyone but his wife. What he saw at last was what Winthrop had tried to point out to him, that he was seeking an unattainable goal, that there was no escape from the dung heap of this earth.

Williams's reaction to this discovery was characteristic: since he could not escape the dung heap, he would embrace it. And so, Winthrop says, "having, a little before, refused communion with all, save his own wife, now he would preach to and pray with all comers."

To Winthrop this liberalism was as ridiculous as the former separatism. Williams's views on civil government had degraded the holy purpose of the state; now he degraded the still holier purpose of the church, welcoming the mixed multitude which he had formerly complained of so bitterly in the churches of England. Many of his followers were as disgusted with his about-face as Winthrop was. It would take another fifty years before a Solomon Stoddard could demonstrate to New England that since perfect purity could not be found in the visible church, the purest course was not to seek it. To Winthrop and to other New England Puritans of the 1630's such was the counsel not of wisdom but of despair and defeat, the very thing to be expected from a man like Williams, who leaped always from one extreme to another.

Winthrop was undoubtedly pained that Massachusetts had been unable to harness the zeal of so godly a man as Williams to the cause the colony was striving for. But he could take pride in the fact that the colony had not been split apart or lured into such an irresponsible pursuit of individual holiness as Williams advocated. The great majority of the population, even the great majority of the Salem church, kept their eyes on the goal that Winthrop had set them.

It was not a goal that any man could reach by himself,

but a common goal which all must seek together, with church and state working side by side. It was a goal of godliness, and it needed godly men to reach it, but not those, like Williams, who pulled too hard and left the rest behind. If such wild ones could not be tamed, it was best to cut them loose, lest they overturn the whole enterprise. Williams had proved impossible to tame. Perhaps if Winthrop, with all his conciliatory skill, had been governor, it might have been done, and Massachusetts would have been the gainer. Since it was not done, the colony was better off without so great a dissenter.

X

Seventeenth-Century Nihilism

On September 18, 1634, two hundred passengers disembarked at Boston's bustling, cluttered landing place and picked their way through the dirty streets. The squalor of the place was enough to make them quail, but they reminded themselves that it was holy ground, where they might worship God without bishops or kings or Romanizing ritual. Among the arrivals who strengthened their resolution with this thought were William Hutchinson and his wife Anne.

Winthrop described Hutchinson as "a man of a very mild temper and weak parts, and wholly guided by his wife." But a man with a wife like Anne Hutchinson could scarcely not have been guided by her. All we know about Anne Hutchinson was written by other hands than hers, for the most part by writers whose main purpose was to discredit her. Yet the force of her intelligence and character penetrate the libels and leave us angry with the writers and not with their intended victim.

Winthrop, who was one of the libelers, tells us at the outset that she was "a woman of a ready wit and bold spirit." This was an absurd understatement. Though Winthrop, in common with his century, believed that women's minds could not stand the strain of profound theological speculation, Anne Hutchinson excelled him not only in nimbleness of wit but in the ability to extend a theological proposition into all its ramifications. And like so many of the men and women of this time—like Roger Williams, for example—she was ready to trust her mind and to follow in whatever path it might lead her. In 1634 the path had led to Boston.

She was not, by intention at least, a Separatist; she had once been tempted in that direction but did not succumb. She had nevertheless determined that she must not attend a church where the minister failed to teach the doctrines of divine grace in their undiluted purity. Until 1633 she had listened to the sermons of the Reverend John Cotton at Boston in Lincolnshire and had known them for true preaching. She had also admired her brother-in-law, the Reverend John Wheelwright. But when Cotton and Wheelwright were silenced by the bishops, "there was none in England," she said, "that I durst heare." After Cotton departed for New England, she persuaded her husband to follow him.

In singling out John Cotton as her spiritual leader, Mrs. Hutchinson showed, by Puritan standards, excellent taste. Cotton had already won a reputation in England before he left, and the Boston church chose him as teacher shortly after his arrival in New England in September 1633. Here his fame rose steadily. Indeed, his wisdom was so revered that Hugh Peter, who was later to be honored as Cromwell's chaplain, urged that Cotton be commissioned to "go through the Bible, and raise marginal notes upon all the knotty places of the scriptures." Nathaniel Ward, the testy pastor of Ipswich, held himself unworthy to wipe John Cotton's slippers. And Roger Williams observed that many people in Massachusetts "could hardly believe that God would suffer Mr. Cotton to err."

Winthrop himself was one of Cotton's admirers and frequently took occasion to record the minister's opinions with approval. He valued most in Cotton what Mrs. Hutchinson did—the man's evangelical preaching of God's free grace. All New England Puritans believed in this doctrine, which they usually described in terms of a covenant between God and man whereby God drew the soul to salvation. Strictly speaking, there was nothing a man could do to lay hold of this "covenant of grace." If God predestined him to salvation, God would endow him with faith and fulfill the covenant. But the doctrine could be applied in a variety of ways, and the New England ministers had been suggesting the need to "prepare" oneself so as to facilitate the operation of God's saving grace when and if it should come.

Under the spell of this suggestion it was easy to develop notions of the kind that good Puritans always denounced as "Arminian"—whenever they could recognize them. Though preachers always took care to state that human efforts counted for nothing in the scale of eternity, it was easy to draw the opposite (Arminian) conclusion from their insistence on "preparation," easy to slip into Arminian ways of thinking without realizing it. The history of New England theology for a century and a half after the founding is the history of this steady tendency toward Arminianism, punctuated by periodic reassertions of the Calvinist dogma of divine omnipotence and human helplessness.

John Cotton was the first of a long line of preachers—among whom the most eminent was Jonathan Edwards—to make this reassertion. He did not make it in the unequivocal terms that Edwards did, and perhaps for that reason he did not end as Edwards did by being expelled from his church. Instead he pulled his congregation back from their Arminian wanderings and won their gratitude. Winthrop counted himself as one of those whom Cotton had rescued. He noted in January 1637, that "the Doctrine of free justification lately taught here took me in as drowsy a condition, as I had been in (to my remembrance) these twenty yeares, and brought mee as low (in my owne apprehension) as if the whole work had been to begin anew. But when the voice of peace came I knew it to bee the same that I had been acquainted with before..." Probably most members of the Boston church reacted to Cotton's preaching as Winthrop did. It woke them from their Arminian napping and sharpened their sense of God's free grace, but it did not make them feel in the end that their previous religious experiences had been false.

But the evangelical preaching of divine omnipotence and human helplessness has always produced extravagant results, for these doctrines may too easily be translated into a denial of any connection whatever between this world and the next. Puritanism allowed only a tenuous connection at best; it allowed a man to look at his life here as evidence of his prospects in eternity, but it gave him no opportunity to affect his eternal condition. When John Cotton warned his listeners away from the specious comfort of preparation and reemphasized the covenant of grace as something in which God acted alone and unassisted, a bold mind might believe that life in this world offered no evidence at all of eternal prospects. And Mrs. Hutchinson was nothing if not bold.

After her arrival in Boston her admission to the church was delayed for a time because one of her fellow passengers had been disturbed by some unorthodox opinions she had expressed on shipboard. But John Cotton evidently recognized her theological talents and her zeal, and within two years she was admitted and won the admiration of a large part of the congregation. It was not uncommon at this time for small groups to hold weekly meetings for religious discussions, in which the sermon of the previous Sunday furnished the starting point. Mrs. Hutchinson, who had gained a wide acquaintance in Boston by serving as a midwife, soon found herself the center of one of these meetings, held in her home. She would explain, to the best of her ability, what her beloved Mr. Cotton had said on Sunday and would then go on to expand some of his doctrines.

In these weekly meetings she carried the principles of divine omnipotence and human helplessness in a dangerous direction, toward the heresy known to theologians as Antinomianism. Since man was utterly helpless, she reasoned, when God acted to save him He placed the Holy Ghost directly within him, so that the man's life was thereafter directed by the Holy Ghost, and the man himself, in a sense, ceased to be. At the same time she concluded that human actions were no clue to the question of whether or not this transformation had taken place. The fact that a man behaved in a "sanctified" manner, breaking none of the laws of God, was no evidence that he was saved. In Puritan terminology this meant that "sanctification" was no evidence of "justification," that men's lives in this world offered no evidence of their prospects in the next. The orthodox Puritans never claimed that the correspondence was perfect: hypocrisy together with the thousand imperfections of human vision could deceive the most skillful examiner. But it was usually possible to recognize sanctification, and that sanctification resulted from justification was not to be doubted at all. Mrs. Hutchinson doubted and denied it. She was, it seemed, an Antinomian.

Winthrop first became alarmed by her teachings in October 1636, a few months after the departure of Roger Williams. He noted her errors and began a list of the awful conclusions that must ensue from them, but stopped and left a large blank in his journal, overcome perhaps by the train of horrors he saw before him. Before they were through with Mrs. Hutchinson the guardians of New England orthodoxy enumerated nearly a hundred dangerous propositions that could be deduced from her views. It is not possible to tell which propositions she actually endorsed and which were simply attributed to her, but the list is a formidable one, and strikes at the heart of the Puritan experiment.

Mrs. Hutchinson's first principle, "that the person of the Holy Ghost dwells in a justified person," was dangerously close to a belief in immediate personal revelation. It threatened the fundamental conviction on which the Puritans built their state, their churches, and their daily lives, namely that God's will could be discovered only through the Bible. In combination with the belief that sanctification offered no evidence of justification, it undermined the whole basis for moral endeavor which Puritan theologians had constructed since the time of Calvin. What reason for a man to exert himself for the right if he may "stand still and waite for Christ to doe all for him"? What reason for a church of saints, if "no Minister can teach one that is anoynted by the Spirit of Christ, more than hee knowes already unless it be in some circumstances"? What reason for a state ruled by the laws of God, if "the Will of God in the Word, or directions thereof, are not the rule whereunto Christians are bound to conforme themselves"?

These views were not necessarily separatist. Rather they were a seventeenth-century version of nihilism. But to make matters worse, Mrs. Hutchinson and her friends developed a new and especially invidious form of separatism, too. Though she denied that sanctification could be evidence of justification, she did maintain that any justified person could discern, presumably at the direction of the Holy Ghost within him, whether or not another person was justified. On the basis of this almighty insight Mrs. Hutchinson and her followers confidently pronounced any person they encountered as "under a covenant of grace" (really saved) or "under a covenant of works" (deluded and damned because relying on good works instead of divine grace), so that "it began to be as common here," Winthrop says, "to distinguish between men, by being under a covenant of grace or a covenant of works, as in other countries between Protestants and Papists." The wholesale destructiveness that might result from Mrs. Hutchinson's self-assurance became apparent when she hinted to her admirers that all the ministers in Massachusetts, with the exception of her two old favorites, John Cotton and John Wheelwright, were under a covenant of works and therefore unfit to preach the gospel.

Winthrop saw trouble ahead when he first took notice of Anne Hutchinson's views in October 1636. The weekly meetings at her house were steadily swelling, and the people who attended them walked the streets of Boston wearing the expression of devotees. Those rapt faces, Winthrop knew, carried a threat to the colony's commission. But there was no law against religious gatherings, and Mrs. Hutchinson was careful to state her heresies in equivocal language. It would be difficult to prove anything against her.

By the end of October 1636, her followers felt strong enough to seek an official spokesman for their doctrines in the Boston church. Because Mrs. Hutchinson was a woman, no one would think of proposing her for a church office, but her brother-in-law would do as well. John Wheelwright had arrived in June, with a reputation as an able preacher and with the additional recommendation of having been silenced by the bishops in England. Mrs. Hutchinson, of course, endorsed him, and he endorsed her. At a church meeting on October 30 it was moved that he be made a teacher, though the congregation possessed two other ministers—John Cotton as teacher and John Wilson as pastor. Winthrop grasped the chance to act and immediately opposed the election of a third minister, particularly one "whose spirit they knew not, and one who seemed to dissent in judgment."

As a member of the church, Winthrop had the right to a voice in its affairs, but no more than any other member, and he was up against a growing majority of the Boston church, which included the largest single concentration of freemen in the colony. He was also up against the popular young governor, Henry Vane, who was on his feet at once to say that Wheelwright's doctrines were no different from those of Cotton. Cotton himself neither admitted nor denied the similarity, but obviously was in sympathy with the majority.

More was at stake here than the welfare of the Boston church, and Winthrop, calling on his own reserve of popularity, was able to persuade the meeting not to elect Wheelwright. But the victory cost him many friends, even though he protested that he meant no personal slight to Wheelwright, and "did love that brother's person, and did honor the gifts and graces of God in him." In the weeks that followed, Wheelwright took himself off to the scattered settlement at Mount Wollaston, leaving behind a congregation that grew ever more resentful of Winthrop and his ally, the pastor John Wilson. Wilson, as pastor, had played second fiddle ever since John Cotton had arrived, but Mrs. Hutchinson's infectious contempt reduced his influence in the congregation to the vanishing point. He and Winthrop were left almost alone to console each other.

Winthrop as usual was sure that people would see things his way if they would only listen to reason, and as usual he set down in black and white the reason he hoped they would listen to. Fortunately, before presenting this document to his opponents he sent a copy to his friend Thomas Shepard, the pastor at Cambridge, who saw at once that Winthrop was no theologian. Though Winthrop knew better than his opponents the necessity of living in this world, he was no match for them in speculating about the next. His arguments, if one may judge from Shepard's criticisms (Winthrop's text is lost), were studded with expressions that smacked of Arminianism; "and so," Shepard warned him, "while you are about to convince them of errours, they will proclayme your selfe to hold foorth worse." Winthrop, who was no Arminian, probably destroyed his composition, and Boston remained deluded and defiant.

Though Winthrop could make no headway within his church, the rest of the colony was beginning to take alarm. The members of the Boston faction, like most religious fanatics, were not content to march quietly along their shortcut to Heaven. They hoped to entice the rest of the colony along it and thought the best way was to visit other congregations and heckle the ministers. This method did not prove as effective as Mrs. Hutchinson's winning words. The General Court began to take notice of the problem, and Governor Henry Vane found his popularity ebbing outside Boston as rapidly as Winthrop's had inside. In a petulant fit of tears Vane offered to resign, and the General Court obligingly agreed to let him. This so alarmed his Boston adherents, who enjoyed having a champion in the governor's chair, that they coaxed him hard to stay, and he finally allowed himself to be persuaded.

By the beginning of 1637 the colony was divided into two hostile camps, the one centering in Boston, the other spread out around it, each constantly sniping at the other. In January the General Court ordered a fast, so that the people might mourn their dissensions. But empty bellies seldom beget brotherly love, and when John Wheelwright showed up at the afternoon lecture by Cotton, he rose up at its conclusion to launch a momentous sermon of his own against those enemies of the Lord who thought that sanctification was an evidence of justification. These holy-seeming men, he said, must be put aside. They were under a covenant of works, and "the more holy they are, the greater enemies they are to Christ." True believers must hew them down: "we must lay loade upon them, we must kille them with the worde of the Lorde."

Wheelwright was speaking figuratively and not actually proposing a bloodbath, but he made it plain that he thought most of the existing ministers and probably most of the magistrates, too, could be dispensed with. Someone took down his words, and at the next meeting of the General Court, in spite of the protests of Vane and a few others, he was convicted of sedition. The sentence was deferred till the following session, which the court appointed to be in Cambridge, away from the immediate source of trouble.

This meeting, held the following May, was the regular time for election of officers. When it assembled, a petition from Boston was presented against the conviction of Wheelwright. Governor Vane wanted to deal with the petition before proceeding to election, but Winthrop and the other magistrates insisted on having the election first. When the votes were cast, it was found that Vane had not only failed of reelection but had been left out of the government altogether. The freemen had finally decided to recall the man who was best qualified to restore the peace. Winthrop was back in the governor's chair with Dudley once again as deputy governor. "There was great danger of a tumult that day," Winthrop noted, "and some laid hands on others," but seeing themselves outnumbered, the Bostonians finally decided that this was not the time to hew down the unholy holy and departed for home.

Winthrop now had the authority to crush the opposition, and it was certainly his inclination to bring the whole unhappy business to as speedy an end as possible. But to suppress or banish so large a segment of the population would be to effect the very separation he wished to avoid. His principal weapon must still be persuasion. Instead of dealing with Wheelwright at once, he again deferred sentence and arranged for a general day of humiliation and for a synod of ministers to be held in the late summer to discuss the points at issue and provide the court with a well-defined statement by which to judge the current heresies. Wheelwright was told that the court was still convinced of his guilt, "but if, upon the conference among the churches, the Lord should discover any further light to them than as yet they had seen, they should gladly embrace it." Nor did Winthrop deal with the opposition for their riotous behavior and insolent speeches on election day. Though there had been ample provocation for an indictment, the court hoped that by refraining from this and by deferring Wheelwright's sentence, "their moderation and desire of reconciliation might appear to all."

The ministers from the beginning had tried to win Cotton away from his heretical admirers, but he held firmly to the top of the fence. He did not endorse Mrs. Hutchinson's consignment of the other ministers to perdition, but he refused to believe that she and Wheelwright held the heresies imputed to them. At the same time he himself disapproved the current doctrine of preparation and maintained that more rigorous views had helped to effectuate a marked awakening of the spirit in Boston.

During the summer months Winthrop's dignity and patience were repeatedly taxed by the sulking saints of that town. Until shamed into it, Boston made no move to provide him with the sergeant halberdiers who customarily accompanied the governor to the first day of General Court and to Sunday meeting. Rather than press the point, he used his own servants and politely declined when at last the town left-handedly offered men but not sergeants. His comings and goings from Boston were also pointedly ignored, in marked contrast to the honor accorded him by other towns, which sent a guard to escort him into and out of their territory. And Henry Vane, until his departure for England on August 3, conducted himself with unabashed schoolboy discourtesy, refusing the invitation to

sit in the magistrates' seats at the Boston church, though
he had sat there ever since his arrival in the colony, refusing to attend a dinner party at Winthrop's home and instead carrying off the intended guest of honor, a visiting
English nobleman, to dine on Noddle's Island with Samuel
Maverick.

Although Winthrop set much store by his official dignity, he did not allow himself to be goaded into further recriminations. Once more he put his pen to work, and this
time Thomas Shepard found little to criticize beyond the
fact that he was too charitable to his opponents. But the
charity was calculated. If he could not win over the leaders of the opposition, he might at least draw away their
less extravagant followers.

At the same time he did not propose to allow them to
increase their numbers by bringing over like-minded
friends from England, where the Reverend Roger Brierly
of Grindleton Chapel had recently been achieving notori-
ety by preaching doctrines similar to those of Mrs.
Hutchinson. Winthrop feared that the Grindletonians, as
Brierly's followers were called, would shortly be gravitat-
ing to Massachusetts, and he accordingly sponsored an order of court forbidding anyone to entertain strangers for
more than three weeks without permission of the magistrates. This arbitrary restriction of immigration was denounced by Henry Vane as unchristian. Winthrop defended it but enforced it with his usual flexibility by
granting the immigrant friends and relatives of Mrs.
Hutchinson and Wheelwright four months in which to decide upon a location for settlement outside the colony.

On August 30 the ministers convened in a synod—all
those of Massachusetts, including Wheelwright and Cotton, together with a delegation from Connecticut. For
twenty-four days they defined to each other the dreadful
doctrines that were polluting the air above Boston, and
reached a remarkable unanimity. Even John Cotton, faced

with a solid phalanx of his colleagues, squeezed his views into line. Wheelwright alone remained aloof. Close to a hundred heretical propositions were meticulously described and condemned, though the synod tactfully declined to attribute them to specific persons. The unanimous opinion of this body of experts must have given pause to many who had flirted with the new ideas, but a hard core of devotees in Boston continued a noisy defiance.

Winthrop could see no further avenue of persuasion and in November decided that it was time for action. Wheelwright was summoned again before the General Court and upon his refusal to give up teaching his heresies was banished. But Winthrop knew that Wheelwright was not the main source of the trouble. When the court had finished with him, they sent for his sister-in-law.

What followed was the least attractive episode in Winthrop's career. Anne Hutchinson was his intellectual superior in everything except political judgment, in everything except the sense of what was possible in this world. In nearly every exchange of words she defeated him, and the other members of the General Court with him. The record of her trial, if it is proper to dignify the procedure with that name, is one of the few documents in which her words have been recorded, and it reveals a proud, brilliant woman put down by men who had judged her in advance. The purpose of the trial was doubtless to make her conviction seem to follow due process of law, but it might have been better for the reputation of her judges if they had simply banished her unheard.

Mrs. Hutchinson confronted them at Cambridge, where magistrates and deputies crowded into the narrow benches of the meetinghouse, the only building of suitable size in the town. The ministers too were on hand, but only as witnesses, for this was a civil court, in which they had no authority. There was no jury, and no apparent procedure. The magistrates (and even some of the deputies) flung questions at the defendant, and exploded in blustering anger when the answers did not suit them. Even Winthrop was unable to maintain his usual poise in the face of Mrs. Hutchinson's clever answers to his loaded questions.

The court was somewhat handicapped, because Mrs. Hutchinson throughout the preceding months had played her hand so cleverly that only minor charges could be framed against her. The court was preparing to deal with all Wheelwright's supporters who had signed the petition in his favor. They would be disfranchised, disarmed, and in some cases banished. But Mrs. Hutchinson had signed nothing and so could be charged only with "countenancing and encouraging" those who did. To this was added the even weaker charge that she held in her home meetings of men and women which were not tolerable or comely in the sight of God or fitting for her sex. Following these was a last and more serious indictment, that she had traduced the faithful ministers of the colony.

The ground of the first charge was that in entertaining seditious persons she broke the Fifth Commandment: she dishonored the governors, who were the fathers of the commonwealth. This was not really a far-fetched interpretation, for the Puritans always justified subordination and subjection to the state on the basis of the Fifth Commandment. But Mrs. Hutchinson's "entertainment" of seditious persons could be considered seditious only by the most tenuous reasoning, and her nimble wit quickly devised a dilemma for the court. "Put the case, Sir," she said to Winthrop, "that I do fear the Lord and my parents, may not I entertain them that fear the Lord because my parents will not give me leave?"

Winthrop was unable to find his way around this logical impasse and took refuge in blind dogmatism: "We do not mean to discourse with those of your sex but only this;

you do adhere unto them and do endeavor to set forward this faction and so you do dishonour us."

The court next called upon her to justify the weekly meetings at her house. In answer she quoted two passages of Scripture: Titus II, 3–5, which indicated that the elder women should instruct the younger, and Acts XVIII, 26, wherein Aquila and Priscilla "tooke upon them to instruct Apollo, more perfectly, yet he was a man of good parts, but they being better instructed might teach him."

There followed this interchange:

COURT: See how your argument stands, Priscilla with her husband, tooke Apollo home to instruct him privately, therefore Mistris Hutchinson without her husband may teach
sixty or eighty.

MRS. H: I call them not. but if they come to me, I may instruct
them.

COURT: Yet you shew us not a rule.

MRS. H: I have given you two places of Scripture.

COURT: But neither of them will sute your practise.

To this assertion Mrs. Hutchinson returned her most withering sarcasm: "Must I shew my name written therein?"

Mrs. Hutchinson was having the best of the argument, but the members of the court were only antagonized by her wit. As they saw it, she was usurping the position of a minister without the authority that a minister possessed from his election by a congregation. Her meetings were a fountain of dissension and separatism for which the community was liable to punishment by the Lord. On this note the court closed the argument: "We see no rule of God for this, we see not that any should have authority to set up any other exercises besides what authority hath already set up and so what hurt comes of this you will be guilty of and we for suffering you."

The greater part of the audience doubtless breathed a

silent "Amen," and the trial moved forward to the final accusation, that she had insulted the ministers. The basis of this charge was a conference held the preceding December between the ministers and Mrs. Hutchinson. In spite of the fact that the conference had been private, and they had encouraged her to speak freely, they did not hesitate now to testify that she had designated them all, with the exception of Cotton and Wheelwright, as laboring under a covenant of works. One minister after another was called forward, and when the court adjourned for the day, the evidence against her on this charge looked overwhelming.

That night she went over some notes taken at the December conference by her most determined opponent, John Wilson. Finding some discrepancy between his notes and the testimony offered in court, she demanded the next morning that the ministers be required to give their evidence under oath. This created a considerable stir, because if the ministers swore to their testimony and it was proved to be wrong, they would be guilty not merely of perjury but of blasphemy, of taking the name of the Lord in vain. After much hemming and hawing by the other ministers John Cotton was called upon for the first time to give his version of the conference. With the tact which had enabled him to retain the favor of both sides he soothed the injured pride of his fellow ministers and then brought his speech to a dramatic close by declaring, "I must say that I did not find her saying they were under a covenant of works, nor that she said they did preach a covenant of works." And though pressed by the other ministers, he stood his ground.

With this testimony the case against Mrs. Hutchinson was about to collapse. The first two specifications against her had been too weakly sustained to warrant more than a serious admonition, and now the revered Mr. Cotton had knocked out the props from under the only remaining charge. The triumph was too much. Hitherto Mrs.

Hutchinson had been on guard and had dexterously parried every thrust against her. Had she been content to hold her tongue at this point, her judges might have felt obliged to dismiss her with a censure. But instead she now proceeded to justify herself by a torrent of divine revelations.

Winthrop tried to stop her, but the floodgates were opened—perhaps by hysteria. Suddenly he must have seen where this outpouring might lead and was silent. The minutes raced by as she described how one thing after another had been revealed to her through scriptural passages thrust into her mind by God. To the Puritans this was an acceptable form of revelation. But then, still to the accompaniment of Biblical citations, she came to the revelation that she would come into New England and there be persecuted, but need fear no more than Daniel in the lions' den. "And see!" she cried, "this scripture fulfilled this day in mine eyes, therefore take heed what yee goe about to doe unto me . . . for I know that for this you goe about to do to me, God will ruine you and your posterity, and this whole State."

Here was the naked challenge. Winthrop and his colleagues believed that the Lord would punish Massachusetts if they *did not* punish Mrs. Hutchinson. Obviously either she or they were deluded, and they asked her "How shee did know that it was God that did reveale these things to her, and not Satan." With a final scriptural flourish to justify what she was about to do and with confidence in the Lord's deliverance, Mrs. Hutchinson at last threw off the confining authority of the Bible and swept arrogantly on.

MRS. H: How did Abraham know that it was God that bid him offer his son, being a breach of the sixth commandment?
COURT: By an immediate voice.
MRS. H: So to me by an immediate revelation.
COURT: How! an immediate revelation?
MRS. H: By the voice of his own spirit to my soul.

Here it was at last, an acknowledgment of the heresy so long suspected. The Lord had indeed disclosed who was deluded, but He had left it to the court to strike her down! Winthrop recorded that "the Court and all the rest of the Assembly (except those of her owne party) did observe a speciall providence of God, that ... her owne mouth should deliver her into the power of the Court, as guilty of that which all suspected her for, but were not furnished with proofe sufficient to proceed against her...." It required only the briefest deliberation for the court to agree that Mrs. Hutchinson's words were sufficient cause for banishment, and when she said, "I desire to know wherefore I am banished," Winthrop gave the shabby final word: "Say no more, the court knows wherefore and is satisfied."

The sentencing of Anne Hutchinson was followed by the disfranchising and disarming of her closest adherents, who might at any moment receive an immediate revelation directing them to kill her judges. Religious enthusiasm was known to produce such results. Fortunately, the number of unwavering Hutchinson disciples was small. Her heretical declaration at the trial had driven off many in disillusionment. Though badly shaken, the Boston church for a time kept dogged faith that the declaration had been the result of unfair pressure and chicanery by the court. But when they sought to satisfy their doubts at a church meeting, Mrs. Hutchinson offered some testimony so obviously contrary to her own previous statements that they could only reluctantly conclude to abandon her. In March 1637, they voted to excommunicate her, and at the end of the month, her banishment having been deferred four months because of the winter and her pregnancy, she departed for Rhode Island, followed by the few faithful.

Winthrop's victory at the trial had been an unsavory triumph of arbitrary power, but happily it represented more than the mere crushing of a helpless woman. When she left, Massachusetts lost a brilliant mind, but God's commission was secured. Even the Boston church recovered from the troubles and was restored to unity. Only a little over a year later Winthrop looked back and congratulated himself on not having withdrawn from the church when every hand was turned against him. "By this time," he writes, "there appeared a great change in the church of Boston; for whereas, the year before, they were all (save five or six) so affected to Mr. Wheelright and Mrs. Hutchinson, and those new opinions, as they slighted the present governour and the pastor, looking at them as men under a covenant of works, and as their greatest enemies; but they bearing all patiently, and not withdrawing themselves, (as they were strongly solicited to have done,) but carrying themselves lovingly and helpfully upon all occasions, the Lord brought about the hearts of all the people to love and esteem them more than ever before, and all breaches were made up, and the church was saved from ruin beyond all expectation; which could hardly have been, (in human reason,) if those two had not been guided by the Lord to that moderation."

Thus the final lesson of the Hutchinson affair was the same lesson that Winthrop had been learning all his life, the importance of not separating.

XI

The New England Way

Massachusetts, then, was not going to crumble into a hundred holy little bands, all looking for perfection in this world and finding it in their own exclusive sanctimoniousness. With the successive expulsions of Roger Williams and Anne Hutchinson, the freemen who had rebuked Winthrop in 1634 demonstrated that their mission in the wilderness was the same as his: to found a society where the perfection of God would find proper recognition among imperfect men. Those who looked for a private heaven on earth might now look in Rhode Island—and much joy to them. Those who cared not for heaven or hell could await damnation in the Old World. Massachusetts, saved from the zealots, would go about the business to which Winthrop had committed it. Here between the Merrimack and the Charles would be a new Israel, where men might worship as God commanded and only as He commanded, where they might obey His laws in peace and be punished when they disobeyed, where they could live in the world as God required but not lose sight of the eternity that lay beyond it.

The freemen had shown their dedication to the goal Winthrop set them, but they still had their own ideas about how to reach it. Though they called for his assistance against Anne Hutchinson, they had no intention of relinquishing the share of power they had won in 1634.

There would be four meetings of the General Court every year, making laws to limit the discretion of the magistrates, and the freemen would be represented by their elected deputies. A benevolent despotism, they were convinced, was not the way to carry out God's commission.

Winthrop disagreed, and so did a number of his fellow magistrates. They could not escape the changes made in 1634, but the settlement of that year had left a great many details of the government untouched, and they hoped that in settling those details they might still retain the kind of paternalistic state in which they believed. Even while they fought for the life of their experiment against Roger Williams and Anne Hutchinson, Winthrop and the freemen wrestled with each other over this problem. It was, of course, the old struggle for power that goes on inside every society, but in Massachusetts the stakes were high. If the people of this colony were to lead the world in establishing the kind of community God demanded, then they could not afford to err. The role of the deputies, of the clergy, of the magistrates, and of the people must be as God would have it; the laws must be His laws; the government must be His government.

The most difficult problem, in Winthrop's view, was that of the deputies. Winthrop had enough political sense to know that they were there to stay, but he could not bring himself to look on them as genuine officers of government. They were, rather, the representatives of the people, and their only role was to keep the government in touch with public opinion. The magistrates, on the other hand, though elected by the same voters, represented not the people but God. Their authority came from Him and not from the men who put them in office.

Winthrop did not want a government entirely free from popular control. In 1630 he had voluntarily abandoned the oligarchy which the charter made possible, and in 1631 he had persuaded the other magistrates to allow popular election of the governor and deputy governor as well as assistants. In 1634 he had been willing to give the people a voice in matters of taxation and land distribution and in the revision of laws they felt unsatisfactory. But he wanted no blurring of the distinction between rulers and ruled. To confound the two would be to make mockery of the authority God gave to rulers. As John Cotton put it, "if the people be governors, who shall be governed?" Moreover, if the purpose of government was to curb human depravity, then it must be set apart from the people and enabled to act upon them with all the majesty of divine sanction. This could never be if the government were run by the people or their deputies, and subject to their every corrupt whim.

The deputies understandably took a higher view of their role and of their competence to fill it than did Winthrop. While he tried to reduce their part in the new government, they did their best to enlarge it. Winthrop began the dispute shortly after his ouster from the governor's chair by claiming for the magistrates (the governor, deputy governor, and assistants) a "negative voice" on all legislation. The freemen wanted laws. Very well, but no law, he said, could be made without the consent of a majority of the magistrates, though all the freemen or their deputies should be for it. The deputies outnumbered the magistrates in the General Court and if allowed to carry measures by a simple majority, they might frustrate the work of the government, that is, of the magistrates, who were the authorized vicegerents of God.

Winthrop assumed that the line between governors and governed ran between the magistrates and the deputies. But he did not rest his case simply on this assumption. The freemen had claimed the charter as the basis of government. To the charter he went, therefore, and came up with the provision that the authority of the General Court was to be exercised by the majority of the members present, "whereof the Governor or Deputie Governor and six of the Assistants, at the least [are] to be seven." This passage, according to Winthrop, was not merely a definition of the quorum necessary to transact business. Rather it was a requirement that every measure have the approval of the governor or deputy governor and six assistants. It meant, in effect, that no law could be valid unless it was accepted by a majority of the magistrates as well as by a majority of the freemen or their deputies.

Since the General Court was the supreme court as well as the supreme legislature of Massachusetts, the negative voice also meant that no final judicial decision could be rendered against the will of the magistrates. That the magistrates should exercise such control seemed desirable to Winthrop for several reasons, foremost of which was that they were admittedly elected as the best qualified men in the colony for wisdom, judgment, ability, and knowledge. It was to the interest of every freeman to choose well, for the magistrates' duties included sitting as judges in the local county courts and in the monthly Court of Assistants where appeals were heard.

The freemen recognized the scarcity of qualified men; they reelected many of the same magistrates again and again. This lack of men with the education, legal training, and experience necessary to fit them to make judicial decisions—or legislative ones—was a constant concern to Winthrop. In 1634 he had tried to bar the freemen from power in the General Court for just this reason. "For the present," he had told them, "they were not furnished with a sufficient number of men for such a business." They had taken their powers anyhow and transferred them to deputies. But the deputies, as a group, were no better qualified than the freemen. These pious but unlearned men were called upon to act as a supreme judiciary without even taking an oath to judge according to the laws of God and of the land (because they were not regular judges). Through the place they occupied in the General Court they enjoyed a power in judicial matters equal to that of the wisest and most learned magistrates in the land. Only by the negative voice could the magistrates prevent them from committing the grossest errors.

Winthrop was not able to get the negative voice accepted without opposition, even though it would guarantee an equal power of veto to the deputies. But the matter was so important to him that he supported it with a vehemence he seldom displayed. When Israel Stoughton, a substantial and straightforward freeman from Dorchester, drew up a list of arguments against it, Winthrop rode him down as "a troubler of Israel" and demanded that the General Court burn his arguments and disbar him from office for three years. Winthrop still had enough prestige to carry this point, but in his vindictiveness against Stoughton he overreached himself. Stoughton, who was an honest and able man, admitted privately that Winthrop was "a man of men," but added wisely, "He is but a man: and some say they have idolized him, and do now confesse their error."

This was in 1635, when the election again left Winthrop out of the governorship. But the troubles with Roger Williams and Anne Hutchinson were now approaching, and many freemen were ready to give the magistrates a stronger hand to deal with separatism. In 1636, after Williams had departed, the General Court confirmed the negative voice by a statute declaring "that noe lawe, order, or sentence shall passe as an act of the Court, without the consent of the greater parte of the magistrates on the one parte, and the greater number of the deputyes on the other parte."

This was not the end of the question. Whenever the magistrates exercised their veto, there was apt to be argument about it, but they clung to their position and in 1644 secured it by a formal division of the General Court into two houses.

Meanwhile Winthrop and those who agreed with him on the desirability of a strong magistracy took advantage of the uproar caused by the Williams episode to inaugurate another device for stabilizing their authority. The meeting of the General Court in March 1636 made provision for the election, as occasion might demand, of "a certaine number of magistrates for the tearme of their lyves, as a standing counsaile, not to be removed but upon due conviction of crime, insufficiency, or for some other waightie cause; the Governor for the tyme being to be always president of this counsaile." It was intended that the council should be drawn principally from ex-governors, and accordingly Winthrop and Dudley were selected as the first members. The following month they were empowered to run the colony in the intervals between meetings of the General Court. This they proceeded to do with a very free hand, for the definition of the council's powers had been left comfortably vague and ambiguous.

Thus the government of Massachusetts still had some of the character Winthrop desired for it when he took office again as governor in 1637. After he succeeded in driving Anne Hutchinson and her followers to Rhode Island, a grateful colony was content for some time to let him manage affairs in his own way, and the General Court rewarded his services with generous grants of land in the new plantation then beginning at Concord. Friends wrote from England, too, congratulating him on his great success in vanquishing the dangerous opinions which had troubled the colony, and Englishmen demonstrated their confidence by coming over in such numbers as had never been seen before, three thousand in the summer of 1638 alone. God manifested His approval in other ways, too. In the spring of 1637, while Winthrop was in the process of subduing Mrs. Hutchinson, the colony became involved in a war against the Pequot Indians. Through the timely warnings of Roger Williams, who was corresponding regularly with Winthrop, and with the assistance of the settlers in Connecticut, who bore the brunt of the fighting, the Pequots were destroyed, virtually the whole tribe killed or captured. Winthrop's earlier reasoning that there was "more than enough" room in New England for both the Indians and the English had given way to his and other Puritans' image of the Indians as instruments of Satan for whom in the end no room need be spared. The English instigation of the war that wiped out the Pequots was another move against Satan to match the defeat of Mrs. Hutchinson.

The abundant evidence of divine favor served to confirm Winthrop in his commitment to a government with wide discretionary powers, dedicated to the enforcement of the laws of God, but not accountable to anyone but God. Whenever his actions as governor were questioned, he would carefully explain why he had done what he did, and might even modify his decisions to meet criticisms, but he never failed to rebuke the questioners. The freemen were for the moment so pleased with his combination of firmness and flexibility that in 1638 and again in 1639 they reelected him in spite of an intention expressed in 1635 to have the office rotate.

But the forces which produced the revolution of 1634 were not extinct. Thomas Dudley still insisted on rigor; and among the freemen new leaders were arising to challenge Winthrop's paternalism. As soon as his three-year disqualification expired, Israel Stoughton was elected an assistant. With him stood Richard Bellingham, one of the original members of the Bay Company, and Richard Saltonstall, the son of an original member.

Bellingham had been a lawyer in England and a member of Charles I's Parliament of 1628. After his arrival in Massachusetts in 1634 he served for a year in the General Court as deputy for Boston and then was made an assistant and treasurer of the colony. He was a mercurial individual, melancholic and impetuous, not Winthrop's idea of a proper magistrate at all. Bellingham had equal misgivings about Winthrop's high notions of governmental authority and, perhaps from his experience in Parliament, had gained high notions of his own about the authority of the people. He and Saltonstall, who was elevated to the magistracy in 1637, generally deserted their colleagues for the side of the deputies whenever there was a dispute.

In spite of these defections, Winthrop might have been able to continue the high-toned government he thought best if he had not met with opposition from another quarter—the clergy. Although no clergyman ever held civil office in seventeenth-century Massachusetts, clerical influence was conspicuous on more than one occasion in reducing the authority of the magistrates and magnifying the liberties of the freemen.

The relationship between church and state was one of the things that the Puritans knew they must get right. They were certain that God had prescribed the terms of it, and they had thought much about it before leaving England, where church and state were confounded at every level from parish to Crown. In Massachusetts the Puritans drew a firmer dividing line between the two than existed anywhere in Europe. The state was still responsible for supporting and protecting the church: as guardian of the divine commission the state must punish heresy like any other sin. And it did so, inflicting loss of civil and political rights as well as other penalties. But in prosecuting heresy it did not operate as the agent of the churches. It formed its own judgments with the aid of a jury or in the General Court, where the respresentatives of the people sat in judgment with the magistrates. The church had no authority in the government and the government was particularly careful not to allow the actions of any church to affect civil and political rights. In England excommunication carried heavy civil disabilities, in Massachusetts none. The right to vote and hold office was not revoked by loss of church membership.

Though the clergy had no political authority of any kind, they did enjoy a very powerful indirect influence. They were highly respected by their congregations, and when unpopular measures had to be adopted, the magistrates counted on their assistance in reconciling people to the necessity of obedience. When a difficult decision had to be made, the magistrates frequently consulted the ministers, who were learned men and wise in the laws of God. In this way, though they were barred from the exercise of authority, a back door was left open through which they could influence state policy.

Normally the magistrates accepted the advice of the clergy, but the magistrates were big enough men in their own right to maintain their independence—as long as the government remained entirely in their hands. The admission of the deputies to the government magnified clerical influence. Thereafter, whenever the deputies and the magistrates were at odds on any question, both sides were tempted to seek the support of the ministers, whose influence on their congregations might swing the balance of power. Had they been ambitious for temporal authority and had their beliefs not forbidden it, the clergy might have won a regular position in the government. They did not attempt to do so; but when they were consulted in disputes between deputies and magistrates, they did not hesitate to throw their weight on one side or the other.

Although for the most part they supported the magistrates, they agreed with the deputies on the need for specific legislation to reduce discretionary authority. Even John Cotton, one of the most consistent supporters of stability in government, one of the most outspoken enemies of "mere democracy," argued that the prerogatives of authority must be clearly limited. "They will be like a Tempest," he said, "if they be not limited: a Prince himselfe cannot tell where hee will confine himselfe, nor can the people tell: But if he have liberty to speak great things, then he will make and unmake, say and unsay, and undertake such things as are neither for his owne honour, nor for the safety of the State. It is therefore fit for every man to be studious of the bounds which the Lord hath set."

With the ministers preaching the limitation of authority and Winthrop insisting on the opposite, the freemen began once more to grow concerned. Everyone admitted that Winthrop was a great man and an excellent governor, but his preeminence made his views seem the more dangerous. Every year brought more Englishmen to Massachusetts, men who had suffered from the discretion of an absolute ruler. In spite of Winthrop's benevolence and wisdom, they felt uneasy for the future.

The ministers continued to worry the subject, and before the election of 1639, some of them tried to persuade the freemen that it was dangerous to keep on reelecting Winthrop to the governorship. Their arguments proceeded, Winthrop wrote, "not out of any dislike of him, (for they all loved and esteemed him,) but out of their fear lest it might make way for having a governour for life, which some had propounded as most agreeable to God's institution and the practice of all well ordered states." Those ministers most sensitive to the dangers of unlimited authority evidently detected that Winthrop himself would not have been averse to a life term. Such was his popularity that they could not prevent his reelection, but they argued the matter so heatedly that many freemen received the impression there was a plot afoot to install a governor for life. As a result, the deputies at the next meeting of the General Court took steps to clip the wings of the Council for Life, established three years before. In their capacity as councilmen Winthrop and his colleagues had been exercising powers that (according to the deputies) they were entitled to exercise only when they sat as magistrates in the

General or Assistants Court. Though the General Court did not abolish the council, they did confine its jurisdiction to a few specifically stated functions: military affairs, the Indian trade, and the customs service.

Winthrop accepted this decision with obvious reluctance, thereby perhaps confirming the fears of the deputies and the clergy that he wanted too much power. Before the next election the ministers busied themselves again to effect his ouster, "fearing lest the long continuance of one man in the place should bring it to be for life, and, in time, hereditary." It took some doing to persuade the people to elect anyone else. "Many of the elders," Winthrop noted, "labored much in it," though without any hard feeling toward him. Meeting in Boston in order to concert their efforts, "they sent some of their company to acquaint the old governour with their desire, and the reasons moving them, clearing themselves of all dislike of his government, and seriously professing their sincere affections and respect toward him." He thanked them, assured them that he understood their motives, and expressed "his unfeigned desire of more freedom that he might a little intend his private occasions"; but he doubtless made plain that he would not refuse if the people chose to call him once again—God intended men to use the talents He gave them.

The man whom the elders had selected as the most likely candidate to beat Winthrop was his old friend and antagonist, Thomas Dudley. By a narrow margin Dudley was elected, and in the following year, 1641, through equally strenuous efforts, Richard Bellingham was chosen by a majority of six votes over Winthrop.

With Winthrop out of the way for two years, the deputies were able to press forward with the project which they had pursued ever since their admission to the government. At their first meeting in the General Court in 1634 they had secured the passage of one or two general laws;

and at ensuing sessions they kept adding more. They wanted as soon as possible a full and explicit body of legislation to restrain the magistrates and to guarantee civil rights and liberties, but they recognized that laws must be carefully drawn, especially in Massachusetts, where every clause must conform to the word of God. As early as 1635 they saw that their own piecemeal efforts would never provide them with an adequate code, and appointed a committee to frame a complete body of laws "in resemblance to a Magna Charta."

The committee, consisting of John Haynes, Richard Bellingham, Thomas Dudley, and Winthrop, never brought in a report. Winthrop was against the whole idea and quarreled with the other members over the question of leniency. The next year the deputies tried again with a mixed committee of magistrates and ministers. This one did produce a code, the work of John Cotton, but the details of it were not altogether pleasing to the deputies. Though Cotton believed in explicit legislation to limit authority, he had as high notions as Winthrop about keeping government stable. He had argued in 1634 for the reelection of Winthrop, and he went a step further in his code by providing that all assistants be elected for life terms. Though the deputies had agreed to establish the Council for Life, this wholesale creation of life tenures was too much for them. Cotton's code was "taken into further consideration" and quietly put on the shelf.

In 1638, after Winthrop had been back as governor for a year, the deputies resumed their efforts. Gradually things began to move, but as slowly as Winthrop could make them, and when Dudley took over again in 1640, no code had been established. Winthrop explained candidly in his journal why he and some of the other magistrates were dragging their feet. It was not, he said, that they wanted no laws at all, but that they wanted the laws to arise out of judicial decisions rather than out of wholesale legislative enactments. Massachusetts was a new country and a new kind of society, dedicated as no other society had been to carrying out God's covenant. Though the terms of that covenant were set down clearly in the Bible, they could not be applied exactly as they had been in Israel. To agree in advance on positive applications would impose an impossible rigidity. God's will would be defeated in the very attempt to carry it out. Much better to leave the magistrates a free hand. Let them search the Scriptures for the proper rule in each case as it arose. The decisions would be recorded, and when a similar case arose in the future, the judges could hark back to it and be guided by it. Through just such precedents the common law of England had arisen. And wise men had even argued that the common law was more binding, more in accordance with God's will, than the statutes enacted by Parliament.

There was another reason, too, why Winthrop disliked legislation: the Massachusetts charter forbade legislation contrary to the laws of England, and the right legislation would have to depart from English law at many points. There was, however, no express limitation on judicial or executive action, and these might escape official notice in England. For example, if Massachusetts simply followed the practice of having civil magistrates perform the marriage ceremony (as the Scriptures, to Puritan eyes, demanded), no one in England need be the wiser. But to pass a law forbidding any but magistrates to perform it would be to invite interference from England, and might lead to revocation of the charter.

Winthrop's arguments were not unreasonable, but they were no answer to the deputies. He spoke of making laws by judicial precedents, but that was exactly what they feared: how could they be sure the precedents would be the right ones? Precedents accumulating slowly, almost surreptitiously, not exposed to public deliberation might be chains to bind the people in slavery. Government existed to control human corruption; but governors were human, and there must be some way of controlling their corruption, too. A code, therefore, the deputies would have, and they finally found the right man to draw it up—Nathaniel Ward of Ipswich.

Ipswich, the second largest settlement in the colony, attracted men of character (including Winthrop's eldest son, John). Nathaniel Ward, like many Puritans and especially those of Ipswich, was an outspoken man. He was older than Winthrop and had behind him ten years of legal training and practice in London, ten years on the Continent, and ten years as rector of Stondon-Massey in Essex. He came to Ipswich at the age of fifty-five in 1634, served as pastor for a couple of years, and then resigned because of ill health but stayed on in the town.

He was no democrat and no demagogue. Before he died he returned to England and dared stand before the House of Commons and denounce it for its treatment of the King. "I see the spirits of people runne high," he observed disapprovingly to Winthrop in 1639, "and what they gett they hould." But the deputies did well in selecting him to draw their code. His legal experience was more extensive than Winthrop's and had probably been gained in the common-law courts, where lawyers learned to match laws against the discretion of the King, and where the people of England were gradually accumulating a heritage of civil liberties. Ward disapproved of giving the people a free hand in the government, but he was clear that "they may not be denied their proper and lawfull liberties."

These liberties, along with the liberties of magistrates, churches, animals, servants, children, and women, he sought to protect in the Body of Liberties, as the code he drafted came to be called. There were a hundred provisions, many of which would have been welcomed by most men in old England, whether Puritan or not—for example, number nine: that "no monopolies shall be granted or allowed amongst us, but of such new Inventions that are profitable to the Countrie, and that for a short time"; or number ten, forbidding feudal restrictions on land: "All our lands and heritages shall be free from all fines and licences upon Alienations, and from all hariotts, wardships, Liveries, Primerseisins, yeare day and wast, Escheates, and forfeitures, upon the deaths of parents or Ancestors, be they naturall, casuall or Juditiall." There would be no Court of Wards and Liveries in Massachusetts. Ward introduced other innovations, too, based on his legal experience, to make Massachusetts judicial procedures simpler than England's. And he guarded the traditional liberties for which Englishmen were even then struggling in the mother country: trial by jury and due process of law.

But the code was not merely a bill of rights to protect the inhabitants of Massachusetts from arbitrary government. It was a blueprint of the whole Puritan experiment, an attempt to spell out the dimensions of the New England way. Trial by jury was part of that way (although the General Court, exercising supreme jurisdiction, operated without a jury) and so was freehold tenure of lands, but only because these practices seemed in accord with the laws of God; for the New England way must be the way God wanted His kingdom on earth to be run, and every law must be measured by His holy word. "No custom or prescription," said the Body of Liberties, "shall ever prevaile amongst us in any morall cause, our meaning is [that no custom or prescription shall] maintaine anythinge that can be proved to bee morallie sinfull by the word of God." And it enumerated all those crimes which the laws of God branded as deserving death: idolatry, witchcraft, blasphemy, murder, bestiality, sodomy, adultery, man-stealing, false witness, and treason. The list included several crimes which were more lightly punished in England, but the very brevity showed that God demanded lesser punishments for most offenses than the King of England did. In England the number of capital crimes amounted to about fifty during the seventeenth century and rose to well over a hundred in the eighteenth.

The Body of Liberties did not describe in detail the machinery of government that had been worked out for God's kingdom in Massachusetts during the preceding ten years. It did not, for example, define the relative authority of deputies and magistrates, which was still a matter of dispute. But it did lay down some general principles of fundamental importance: it reaffirmed the decision of 1634 in a provision stating the right of each town to choose deputies for the General Court; it guaranteed the right of freemen to elect all officers of government annually; and it defined the relationship of church and state in unmistakable terms. The state could establish Christ's religion in every church, and it could "deale with any Church member in a way of Civill Justice, notwithstanding any Church relation, office or interest." The church, or rather any particular church, could "deale with any magestrate, Deputie of Court or other officer what soe ever that is a member in a church way in case of apparent and just offence given in their places, so it be done with due observance and respect," but "no church censure shall degrad or depose any man from any Civill dignitie, office, or Authoritie he shall have in the Commonwealth." In other words, a church might censure or excommunicate a magistrate (who happened to be a member) for some improper magisterial action, but the excommunication would not affect his authority or the validity of what he did.

The code also stated some of the principles governing the special institution that the people of Massachusetts had developed to replace the parishes and boroughs and manors from which they had come. In these institutions of English local government, church and state were hopelessly entwined. In order to separate them and also do away with archaic forms of land tenure, it was necessary to construct an altogether new kind of unit, a unit which would be a parish without church officers, a borough without aldermen, a manor without a lord. The New England town was not built after any preexisting pattern, nor were all towns alike. But in the course of a decade towns had somehow come into being, and some common features had emerged to which the Body of Liberties gave the sanction of law: the freemen of every town should have power to make bylaws (not contrary to the laws of the colony) and could also "choose yearly or for lesse time out of themselves a convenient number of fitt men to order the planting or prudentiall occasions of that Town." These "select persons" should not exceed nine in number and were to do nothing contrary to written instructions given them by their constituents. A unique form of local government had been created.

After much discussion and revision the code of liberties was finally accepted by the General Court in December, 1641. Winthrop recorded the fact in his journal without comment. He would doubtless have been happier if its provisions had been left unexpressed, but he probably found little to quarrel with in the substance of them. They defined the New England way for all to see, and if this might bring trouble, it might also prompt the world to imitation.

The freemen, in any case, were pleased to have things written out. There was still, of course, a great deal left undecided. Nothing, for example, had been said about the education of children, and in the following year the General Court made it a law that all parents see that their children be taught to read. A later enactment provided for free public schools. Many more laws would be needed in the coming years; but with the Body of Liberties established, the freemen felt safe in summoning Winthrop back as their leader. In May 1642, they returned him to the governorship and kept him there, in spite of occasional protests by clergymen, for most of the remainder of his life.

Meanwhile, during the time Nathaniel Ward was constructing the Massachusetts Magna Charta, things began to happen in the rest of the world that would alter the significance of everything Winthrop and his colony had done or could ever do.

XII

New England or Old

Winthrop was not merely being polite when he told the ministers before the 1640 election that he would be glad to retire from the governorship and attend to his private affairs. Though he enjoyed using his political talents and would doubtless have taken office if elected, his private affairs badly needed looking after. For the better part of ten years he had been devoting himself to the public. During that time, to judge from the surviving correspondence, everyone in England who wanted a favor done called on Winthrop to do it. A son is going astray. Won't Winthrop keep an eye on him? A mother needs her boy back in England. Won't Winthrop get him released from his master and ship him home? A father is worried because his son intends to marry a New England lass though a match is already arranged back in England. Will Winthrop please talk to the boy and make him give up this foolishness? As often as not the writers were people Winthrop had never heard of before.

The multitude of smaller problems, combined with the larger affairs of state, left little time for the management of his own concerns. The General Court usually paid him one hundred pounds a year while he was governor, but this hardly covered his expenses, and he had to rely on the income from various lands he had acquired, mostly by gift of the General Court. In the 1630's land was the principal source of wealth in New England, land where cattle could be raised and crops grown. Land, moreover, was the kind of wealth that Winthrop understood and valued. He had two or three thousand acres in various towns, but his most cherished possession was Tenhills Farm, located in what is now Medford. Because of his involvement in public affairs Winthrop could not himself supervise the working of this or his other holdings so he had to hire an overseer. Unfortunately, he picked the wrong man.

James Luxford was an ingratiating character, full of earnestness and humility, so plausible that Winthrop did not discover his incompetence until the man had all but ruined him. Though Luxford was ultimately convicted of bigamy, lying, and forgery, the damage he did Winthrop was more the result of foolishness than of duplicity: in selling or exchanging the produce of Winthrop's lands and in hiring laborers, he made incredibly bad bargains. Perhaps he was overcome with the importance of being the governor's steward and emphasized his position by handing out his master's funds with regal largess. In any case, Winthrop discovered what was happening only after Luxford had contracted debts amounting to twenty-five hundred pounds in his name, with payment agreed upon in corn or cattle valued considerably lower than the market price.

Winthrop was annoyed and hurt that his creditors had taken advantage of his steward, but he did not shirk the responsibility. His house in Boston and many of his lands went up for sale. The General Court donated three thousand more acres to his wife (probably to keep them from being attached by his creditors), and the people of the colony took up a collection and handed him nearly five hundred pounds. His old friends in England, Brampton Gurdon and Sir Nathaniel Barnardiston, wrote offering to lend him money, and though his estate was long in recovering, he was soon out of danger.

Winthrop met his financial crisis as calmly as he met all difficulties. It did not sour him on New England or New Englanders. He was as certain now as he had been in 1630 that the Lord had brought him to a good land. Nor was his confidence in Massachusetts shaken when, shortly after, the whole colony faced an economic crisis as grave as his own.

While Winthrop was beginning to set his own house in order, Charles I of England was trying to set the British Government in order. After affronting the Puritans in England and Scotland for eleven years by silencing the ministers they loved and enforcing the rituals they abhorred, he finally met open defiance in May 1640, when he attempted to impose the Anglican prayer book in Scotland. Charles did not have men or money to put down the rebellion and summoned Parliament, which had been suspended for the past eleven years, to his aid. The end of their long enforced vacation found the House of Commons as much against him as ever. Charles dissolved them almost at once, but the people of England knew that he could not go on much longer without them. A Scottish army was assembling; by the end of the summer it was ready to move against him. In November, Parliament was in session again at Westminster, and did not rise until after Charles's head fell from the block some eight years later.

The events that began in May 1640 had repercussions in Massachusetts almost as profound as in England. Already in the summer of 1640, while the Scots were gathering and the King was hopefully searching for a way to stop them, New England began to feel the change. Ships arrived from England as before, and they brought the usual cargoes of British goods, but precious few immigrants to buy New England's goods. Englishmen had seen that the King was going to have his way no longer. The Great Migration to New England was over. And so was the peculiar prosperity New England had been enjoying.

The lumber and crops and cattle which the colonists had prepared for the annual horde of newcomers lay unsold. By October prices began to fall. When they stopped falling two years later, most crops were worth little more than half what they had been, and cattle were down from twenty or twenty-five pounds a head to eight, seven, or even six.

The crisis was more than economic, for the summoning of Parliament in England and the end of the Great Migration posed a question that went far beyond the simple one of how the colony was to survive economically. The deeper question was whether the colony ought to survive.

Massachusetts had been founded as a refuge for true religion when truth seemed ready to expire in England. Winthrop and others like him had persuaded themselves to come because it seemed that the cause of God could best be served, for the time at least, in New England. But did not opportunity now look eastward? Truth had indeed been preserved in Massachusetts: pure churches had been organized, and valuable experience gained in conducting them according to the word of God. Civil government too had been properly managed, free from the corrupting influence of courtiers and prelates. But now perhaps the time had come to make old England new. Perhaps Massachusetts had served its purpose and the settlers should return to lead their countrymen in reformation of church and state.

As the original exodus to New England had been reinforced by economic depression in England, so now the desirability of returning home seemed to be argued by economic difficulties in New England. The ships that arrived with English goods began to carry more passengers back to England than they brought with them. Probably many were faint of heart, ready to give up when the going got rough. But among them were some of the colony's leaders, men of standing and education who saw greater opportunities for service in England than in the declining refuge in the wilderness. A hundred and fourteen men with university training are known to have been in New England in 1641. During the next year at least fourteen of them returned. In that year Harvard College, which had been founded to supply the colony with civil and religious leaders, produced its first graduating class. There were nine in it, but seven of the nine eventually left Massachusetts, and so did most of the other students who graduated during the next eight years. Back to England they went, for the most part, to speed the good cause there.

The General Court itself could not ignore its responsibilities in the new situation. By the spring of 1641 it appeared that Charles's new Parliament was prepared to proceed with the work of Reformation, stalled since the early years of Elizabeth's reign. It was only proper that Massachusetts should offer advice and assistance, and two prominent ministers, Thomas Welde and Hugh Peter, both of whom had taken an active part in subduing Mrs. Hutchinson, were selected to carry the wisdom of the colony back to the mother country. The General Court did not intend that they should be heralds of a general return to England; they were also supposed to seek financial aid for hard-pressed Massachusetts. Nevertheless, the colony was looking toward England as never before.

In this new orientation Winthrop could scarcely escape the pull of old ties and old responsibilities. For ten years he had been insisting that the people of Massachusetts keep their horizons wide. He had fought separatism in every form and sought always the large view. Did not the large view now require that England come first and Massachusetts second? Many of his old friends and associates were in Parliament, and Sir Nathaniel Barnardiston, who sat for Suffolk, wrote to Winthrop in words that struck home: "Now we see and feele how much we are weakned by the loss of those that are gonn from us, who should have stood in the gapp, and have wrought and wrasled mightely in this great busines." Winthrop had come to Massachusetts to preserve the truth and to exercise a talent for public service that would have been left to decay in England. Now the road was open once more. England needed him. Should he not be the first to go?

He did not go, and neither did most of the others. Though there was a steady trickle of settlers back to England in the 1640's, it never rose to more than a trickle. Most of those who had carved homes out of the wilderness preferred to go on living in them. Most of those who had built pure churches where none had stood before preferred to go on worshiping in them. Though the settlers were fond of retailing the hardships they had suffered in the wilderness, New England had become something more than a temporary refuge for them—and for Winthrop as well as the rest. Much as he strove to keep his horizons open, the landscape of Massachusetts had eaten into his heart and was pushing out the dear images of England that once reigned there. The "faire levels of good meadow," the salt marshes with their "fine, benty grasse," the open woods where a man could ride freely on horseback—these were dimming the memory of the hop yards and pastures and plowlands of Groton.

Winthrop had never allowed himself to be governed by such attachments. Nor did he now. New England was a good land, yes. But he had thought England a good land too and left it on a mission which still engaged him. If some of his friends considered the mission accomplished, he knew better. The purpose of New England was to show the world a community where the laws of God were followed by church and state—as nearly as fallible human beings could follow them.

It was true that this purpose had so far been achieved. Massachusetts came as close as men could come to the kingdom of God on earth. But this was not a business of shooting at the mark and, having struck it, retiring in glory.

God's commission to Massachusetts carried no terminal date. To build a society so near to what God demanded and then abandon it would exhibit nothing but the usual story of human corruption. Massachusetts must go on in the ways of godliness and stand as a permanent example of how much could be accomplished in this world.

It might well be that England was now ready to be salvaged from the mire of sin and corruption, and Winthrop was ready and eager to offer her the benefit of what New England had learned in ten years. He refused, however, to contemplate the dissolution of his solid achievement in favor of the mere prospect of reform in the mother country. And events justified him. Though Parliament forged ahead rapidly in its assault on the prelacy, it was one thing to expel a Roger Williams from the Bay Colony and quite another to cast down a Charles Stuart or a William Laud. The King of England did not give up without a fight, and in spite of his errors many Englishmen were ready to fight by his side. Early in 1642 civil war began.

War was not to be avoided in a righteous cause, but the war aims of those who fought against the King were not what Winthrop or other New Englanders could approve. They applauded the end of bishops and archbishops, of Romanizing rites and rituals; but their views of what should follow the destruction differed from anything the English reformers proposed.

As far as the English were concerned, there seemed to be only two alternatives. The first was Presbyterianism. A large proportion of English Puritans had always been Presbyterians, and as long as the bishops were in the saddle, Congregational Puritans had gladly joined hands with Presbyterians. But even then there had been occasional quarrels. Several New England ministers retained bitter memories of one that took place in Holland, in the 1620's and early 1630's, when a Presbyterian had betrayed them to the prelates.

Holland in those years had been the home of many Englishmen, who lived there as agents for mercantile firms, as volunteers in the Dutch wars against Spain, or as refugees from Anglican religious policy. Among these expatriates, Congregationalism was predominant, and under the Dutch policy of toleration they were able to set up their own churches, where several able young ministers gained experience in presiding over a truly independent congregation. But the long arm of Bishop Laud reached eventually to Holland, and when he began to investigate the Englishmen who were defying him abroad, a Presbyterian minister turned informer and intrigued against his Congregational brethren. The congregations were broken up, and the ministers were obliged to seek refuge elsewhere. They found it in New England, where they and their friends saw to it that Presbyterianism gained no foothold.

In England, however, it had remained strong, and among the members of Parliament it was stronger than Congregationalism. It was also better organized. Congregationalists, opposed to centralization and lacking the kind of control that Winthrop exercised in Massachusetts through the civil government, quickly succumbed to the explosive force of separatism. While the bishops ruled the church, Congregationalists developed their private creeds and, once Anglican control was lifted, proliferated in a hundred different directions. Some were Antipedobaptists; some were Antinomians; some were Socinians. They had in common only a belief in the independence of each congregation, and they came to be known in England as independents. Perhaps the greater part of them adhered to the kind of Congregationalism that was practiced in New England, but more and more they espoused a doctrine which New England could not abide: toleration. This was, in fact, the only policy in which they could see a chance for their own survival, the only policy in which they could join against the Presbyterians.

The alternative to Presbyterianism in England then was a Congregationalism in which each church was free to revel in whatever heresy it chose. Instead of admiring the New Englanders for achieving uniformity, the English Congregationalists proceeded to scold them for being intolerant, and to convert them if they went back to the mother country. Hugh Peter, sent by Massachusetts to help guide the English Reformation, was himself transformed. The man who had hammered relentlessly at Anne Hutchinson was shortly addressing counsels of toleration to his Massachusetts constituents.

The New Englanders were as bewildered as they were outraged. As one friend observed sadly to Winthrop, "This is not a tyme of Reformation but of liberty of conscience: I beleeve," he added, "by that tyme they see a litle more of the lawlessenesse of liberty of conscience, they will change their judgments."

He was wrong, of course. English Congregationalists did not change their judgments. Winthrop had been able to prevent in Massachusetts the development that was now beyond control in England. He had contained separatism and held his holy experiment together, sifting out into Rhode Island the extremists who were beyond recovery. No one could achieve such a thing in England, and hardly anyone, among the Congregationalists at least, wanted to.

All the more reason, then, for keeping Massachusetts true to her holy commission. If England must be the home either of Presbyterianism or of toleration, there would still be need in the world for New England, and there would still be need in New England for Winthrop.

Winthrop stayed on, therefore, and guided Massachusetts through new perils in a world that grew more and more alien. There was first of all the great economic depression to be faced. The colony had always depended heavily on manufactures from abroad, but after 1640 it could no longer afford to buy them. The settlers met the situation partly by trying to make as many of their own goods as possible. The law against monopolies was overlooked in order to encourage entrepreneurs who undertook to produce iron and salt. Men who had worked at textiles in the old country began to manufacture them here. But home manufactures did not begin to solve the problem. The only real solution was to find a foreign market for the Massachusetts goods which formerly had been sold to the annual horde of immigrants. Fishermen expanded their activities to produce an export; shipwrights speeded up their work; and soon New England vessels loaded with fish and hides and cattle and lumber were nosing down the creeks and rivers to seek markets from Nova Scotia to the West Indies and even to Spain, Portugal, and the Azores. New England boys learned to walk familiarly in the streets of strange places with outlandish names—Fayal, Funchal, Teneriffe, Málaga—and came home with good sack and Madeira to gladden the hearts of their countrymen and stiffen the colony's sagging economy.

In the years ahead there were also internal problems: the deputies continued to press for more legislative and judicial authority, more laws, and more limitations on the magistrates; Winthrop continued to work in the opposite direction; and occasionally there were hot words on both sides. But the critical problems of the 1640's were not domestic. The principal threat to the success of Massachusetts, to the kind of success that Winthrop at least wanted, came no longer from internal division. Separatism was still the problem, but a separatism moved by fear, disdain, and distrust of the outside world. Winthrop's talent for public service, his realism in not seeking perfection were never more needed and never used to better effect than in his direction, during the remainder of his life, of the foreign policy of Massachusetts.

XIII

Foreign Affairs

Until 1640 the people of Massachusetts had the fraternal and exciting sense of leading the sinful world back to God. They were surveying a path into the future, a glorious godly future for all mankind to share. But when they turned to beckon England onward, they found themselves suddenly alone in the wilderness. History had turned a corner in pursuit of toleration, and their well-marked route to the kingdom of God on earth became a historical dead end.

As soon as they were aware that the world refused to be led in their direction, in fact had its back turned and was not even looking at them, the urge was born in many to turn their own backs on the world. And the urge was strengthened by the fact that they no longer received a yearly supply of new men with new ideas. Hitherto the immigrants had served as a regular injection of new blood to fight the infection of provincialism. With the supply cut off, the colony nursed its righteousness unchallenged by the irritating presence of newcomers with their own ideas of the good life. Massachusetts was safe from new Separatists, but safe at the risk of succumbing to a new separatism, the separatism of a whole people lost in satisfaction with their own collective holiness and determined to preserve the perfection of their own state by shunning all contaminating foreign contacts.

This kind of separatism wore the appearance of virtue. Just as selfishness looks virtuous when expanded into patriotism, so separatism seemed less separate when indulged in by a whole people. What is wrong in an individual sometimes appears right in a nation—at any rate in one's own nation.

Though Winthrop was an expert at detecting and suppressing separatism in himself and in others, he had been so successful in keeping Massachusetts true to her commission, and the rest of the world was so laggard in following her example, that even he sometimes succumbed to thinking of New England as God's only residence. The pages of his journal frequently depicted the outside world (outside New England) as a sink of iniquity where good men (from inside New England) ventured only at their peril. For instance, he accepted without question the rumor that a certain New Englander who had gone to Virginia was "given up of God to extreme pride and sensuality, being usually drunken, as the custom is there." This particular person had already begun to tread the downward path in Massachusetts, but the casual indictment of Virginia showed clearly what Winthrop thought of that colony. The fate of the man's wife, who left to join him, was equally indicative: "Her friends here persuaded [i.e., urged] her to stay awhile, but she went notwithstanding, and the vessel was never heard of after." In a time when sudden death was thought to spell the judgment of heaven, Winthrop was able to discern God's favor to His chosen people and His displeasure with the rest of the world in every report that reached him from abroad.

God's favor, in Winthrop's mind, included Plymouth, Connecticut, and New Haven, as well as Massachusetts. These four colonies (but not Rhode Island) were embarked on the same enterprise, and in 1643 they joined in a confederation against hostile Indians and against possible attack by the people "of several nations and strange languages" who lived on either side of them. They felt little bond with any other Puritan settlements in other parts of the world. The sponsors of Providence Island in the West Indies were able to persuade a few New Englanders to depart for their tropical paradise, but Winthrop noted pregnantly how God allowed some of the emigrants to be captured by the Turks, while others arrived to find the island in the hands of the Spaniards. A similar settlement in the Bahamas fell prey to heresy. All in all it was apparent to Winthrop and his companions that God's favor in the seventeenth century after Christ was confined pretty much to New England and even there did not extend to Rhode Island.

This provincial self-righteousness—should we call it patriotism?—was not identical with isolationism. But the frame of mind which produced one could easily produce the other, and in many New Englanders it did. In Winthrop it did not. In spite of his conviction that Massachusetts enjoyed God's special favor he never forgot the great lesson of his early life, that the world was not to be escaped. However lost in sin, it was God's world and man's, to be lived in and lived with. Though its evils might infect the holy community, that danger, like all temptations to sin, must be faced, not avoided. Purity must not be sought at the expense of charity.

As Winthrop had learned this principle better than most of his countrymen, he was quicker than they to detect and condemn isolationism. He expressed his disapproval, for example, when the General Court refused an emergency appeal by Virginia for powder and shot to use against an Indian attack. The fact that Massachusetts was herself "weakly provided" with powder and that the Virginians were weakly provided with righteousness did not constitute a sufficient excuse for turning them away empty. God showed His displeasure with New England's arrogance when seven months later Boston's powder house took fire and went sky-high in an explosion that rattled windows as far as Cambridge.

In the domestic crises of the 1630's the freemen and their deputies had demanded rigid standards of righteousness. In the 1640's it was again the deputies, in alliance with the ministers, who forgot the requirements of charity and exhibited the most doctrinaire isolationism. An example was their insistence on keeping the law against strangers. In the Antinomian crisis of 1637 Winthrop had approved a law requiring governmental permission for the entertainment of strangers. The purpose had been to prevent any new accession of strength to Mrs. Hutchinson's party, and Winthrop had defended the law ardently against the attacks of young Henry Vane. With the end of the Antinomian danger and the development of foreign trade, a number of merchants petitioned for repeal of this law and also of another that the General Court had subsequently made for the banishment of Baptists. Winthrop was ready to go along with the petition, but the ministers worked up the deputies and a number of the magistrates against it. A counterpetition was circulated, and the General Court gave out its answer that the laws in question "should not be altered at all, nor explained."

How such laws could operate to the detriment of God's truth Winthrop pointed out in the case of an English ship captain who arrived in Boston and began to voice heretical opinions. John Cotton went to work on the man and was well on the way to bringing him around to othodoxy when it became necessary, according to the law, to require his departure, though he had planned to stay the winter. "This strictness," said Winthrop, "was offensive to many, though approved of by others. But sure the rule of hospitality to strangers, and of seeking to pluck out of the fire such as there may be hope of to be reduced out of error and the snare of the devil, do seem to require more moderation and indulgence of human infirmity where there appears not obstinacy against the clear truth." Massachusetts could no longer hope to evangelize the world, he realized, but she could at least try to save the strangers whom God deposited on her shores.

Winthrop had many more occasions to notice how self-righteousness extinguished charity. It also blinded men to realities. He knew that New England depended on the outside world in its new economy, and his heart was gladdened every time another ship splashed off the ways at Boston to carry New England codfish to markets where idolatrous Roman Catholics paid good money for them. He also knew, what a good foreign minister had to know, that righteousness endangered his community when it produced a blind and undiscriminating defiance to surrounding evils. Thus, when his colleagues refused to aid Rhode Island against the Indians, he remarked that it was an error in state policy, for though the Rhode Islanders were "desperately erroneous and in such distraction among themselves as portended their ruin, yet if the Indians should prevail against them, it would be a great advantage to the Indians, and danger to the whole country by the arms, etc., that would there be had, and by the loss of so many persons and so much cattle and other substance belonging to above 120 families. Or, if they should be forced to seek protection from the Dutch, who would be ready to accept them, it would be a great inconvenience to all the English to have so considerable a place in the power of strangers so potent as they are."

Winthrop saw what few men in any age have learned, that the foreign policy even of the holiest state must support one evil in order to suppress a worse one. Because it requires uncommon wisdom to recognize this fact, and still greater wisdom to choose rightly among the manifold evils of the world, foreign affairs have always suffered when exposed to the undiscriminating zeal of legislative assemblies. Winthrop had frequent cause to regret the increased power of the deputies, for the zeal of the deputies and sometimes even of the magistrates against all outlanders was a constant handicap to him in handling foreign affairs.

His most daring foreign adventure was in playing off two Frenchmen against each other. Charles de Saint Étienne de la Tour and Charles de Menon, Sieur d'Aulnay de Charnisé (names which New Englanders reduced to "Latour" and "Daulnay" or "Dony"), both claimed the governorship of Acadia. The ministers of Louis XIII had commissioned both of them at different times and neglected to define their respective jurisdictions. As a result, they contended like two warlords for control of New Brunswick and Nova Scotia, and sometimes extended their raids to the English fishing settlements on the Maine coast.

Massachusetts became involved in this French feud on a pleasant June day in 1643 when Winthrop, his wife, and two of his sons were enjoying a family excursion to their island, known as the Governor's Garden, in Boston Harbor. Their holiday was suddenly interrupted by a woman hurrying toward them from the shore where she had beached her small boat in terror at the sight of a great French ship. The vessel, she gasped, had already passed the fort on Castle Island at the entrance of the harbor. And there, to prove her words, came the ship; then a shallopload of Frenchmen headed in to the Governor's Garden, and in a moment Winthrop found himself face to face with La Tour.

No armed ship had ever before come to challenge the safety of Boston, and an economy-minded General Court had allowed the walls of the harbor fort to crumble and had even decided, only a few months before, to keep no garrison there. Now within the harbor, unchallenged and unopposed, lay a foreign ship, and the governor was at her mercy.

The sight of the French ship sent the men of Boston and

Charlestown hurrying to arms. Three shallops were just setting out to the rescue—they would have been easy targets for the Frenchmen—when Winthrop and La Tour, apparently on friendly terms, came ashore. Fortunately La Tour had no hostile intentions, toward Massachusetts at least. He had come, rather, in search of aid against his rival.

New Englanders had no love for either of these idolators, but of the two, D'Aulnay was the more aggressive and more prone to attacking English settlements. In La Tour's arrival at Boston, Winthrop saw an opportunity to check D'Aulnay's growing power at low cost. Though wary of becoming too deeply involved in what might prove to be the losing side of a family quarrel, Winthrop was even more concerned to keep the quarrel alive and not have to face D'Aulnay alone. Accordingly he decided, with the approval of such of the magistrates as he could round up for consultation, to give no direct aid—this would have required approval of the other colonies that had joined Massachusetts in the new confederation—but to let La Tour hire any ships and men he could in Boston. The decision was satisfactory to the Frenchman, and he gave evidence of his good faith by accepting lodgings in the town, where a colonial guard of honor attended him, the honor for him and the guard, one suspects, for the colony. He stayed for a month and managed to acquire four ships, a pinnace, and seventy men in addition to the one hundred forty Frenchmen he had brought with him.

It was a risky business for Winthrop, not only because of the danger of reprisal from D'Aulnay, but also because the presence of one hundred forty armed French Catholics in Boston scandalized the whole colony, especially when it was made known that they would be allowed to perform maneuvers on training day, along with the local militia. John Endecott wrote Winthrop from Salem, "I feare we shalle have little comfort in having any thing to doe with theise Idolatrous French." And one minister warned darkly that before training day ended, blood would be spilled in Boston.

When training day came, the Frenchmen politely watched the colonial soldiers go through their exercises in the forenoon, and in the afternoon the whole town assembled again on the common to watch the visitors drill. The performance was "very expert," but at one point it appeared that all the bloody predictions were about to be fulfilled. In the midst of an exercise with muskets, the Frenchmen dropped their guns, threw off their bandoliers, and, brandishing their swords, charged across the field toward the spectators. They stopped short of the astonished and fleeing crowd, who then realized this was merely a routine maneuver. Nevertheless, it seemed to New Englanders a bad sort of joke. On the day the Frenchmen left, Winthrop received a formal protest against his too cordial treatment of them, signed by three magistrates and four ministers. In the next two elections he was left out of the governorship (but retained as deputy governor).

Actually Winthrop had picked the losing side. In spite of his assistance, La Tour was unable to stand up against D'Aulnay. The victor, however, did not prove so dangerous a neighbor as had been feared, perhaps because Winthrop had shown him that Massachusetts was not a province to be trifled with. Winthrop was ultimately able to negotiate peace with him and sweetened the bargain by the gift of a sedan chair (a white elephant which Winthrop had himself received as a gift from a visiting privateer, who had captured it on a Spanish ship).

In playing this daring game with the two Frenchmen, Winthrop showed his readiness to do business even with men of whose religion he wholly disapproved. It did not follow that he was ready for friendship with any foreign power. To the south of New England the settlements sponsored by the Dutch were Protestant and therefore presumably more worthy of friendship than the French to the north. But Winthrop was cautious to avoid entangling alliances with them. If they got themselves in danger from the Indians, he was willing to lend a hand; and he was not above making rhetorical appeals to their common Protestantism when a dispute arose, but be did not allow himself to be moved very far by similar appeals from the Dutch governor.

Winthrop knew what he was doing. Within his colony he must indeed make war on all evil and nourish all good; but the special commission of Massachusetts did not require vain warfare against every evil power in the outside world, nor did it require help to every good power if such help might endanger the safety of God's model kingdom on earth. In a word, Winthrop did not allow his foreign policy to become a simple projection of domestic policy. Foreign policy and domestic policy were interdependent, but the two were not identical.

In dealing with the French and Dutch it was easy enough to keep them straight. But another department of foreign affairs proved more difficult to handle, one in which domestic and foreign matters were so closely blended that even the expert hand found difficulty separating them. The relations of Massachusetts with England were so complicated by emotional, religious, and legal ties that no one could say quite what they were or what they ought to be.

Winthrop was ready to stick with Massachusetts and carry on the mission begun in 1630, whatever might happen elsewhere. But neither he nor anyone else could erase the years spent in England or remain neutral when King and Parliament divided in civil war. Most New Englanders sympathized with Parliament, but some found it hard to give approval to men who raised a hand against their king. Winthrop recorded one such case, that of a deputy from Watertown, who had been among the first settlers there. Though the man allowed himself to be persuaded "that those of the parliament side were the more godly and honest part of the kingdom," he still felt that "if he were in England, he should be doubtful whether he might take their part against their prince." On the other hand, there was no doubt in his mind about the supreme importance of Massachusetts: "If the king or any party from him should attempt any thing against this commonwealth, he should make no scruple to spend estate and life and all in our defence against them."

Others were less certain about their ultimate loyalty. Some went to England for the express purpose of fighting their king, but of these, several were disillusioned and came back to Massachusetts. Some continued to think of England as home, and the whole colony held fast days from time to time, to mourn for the troubles across the sea. Indeed, they mourned so frequently that Winthrop eventually became impatient with them. There was no doubt in his mind that ultimate loyalty belonged to Massachusetts.

The relationship to England was more than a matter of loyalties. There was also the legal and constitutional question, which was never merely academic. Winthrop had once rested the authority of his government on a social compact, the agreement of October 1630; but the freemen, seeking more power for themselves, repudiated the compact and insisted on the charter as their constitution. Under it they enjoyed virtual self-government; there was no effective way in which England could control them. Yet they could not deny that the source of whatever authority their government now possessed was in England.

Winthrop was content to acknowledge the subordination of Massachusetts to England, provided the mother country made no serious attempt to recover the powers which the King had so freely given. In the 1630's, when Charles was trying to consolidate his authority, he had attempted to recover the Massachusetts charter. Winthrop at that time responded with evasive answers, until Charles lost patience and obtained a judgment in court, revoking the grant. The court evidently thought it necessary, however, to regain actual possession of the charter. Winthrop had no intention of giving it up, nor did the members of the General Court; they had taken advantage of the delay "to hasten our fortifications." Massachusetts was saved from the necessity of outright defiance only by the calling of the Long Parliament in 1640.

When that body met, Winthrop had heard from friends who were sitting in it that the members were well disposed toward Massachusetts and would be glad to protect the colony against the King. After consulting the other magistrates, Winthrop decided to let things ride for the time being. The King had his hands full at home now, anyhow; and "if we should put ourselves under the protection of the parliament," Winthrop had reasoned, "we must then be subject to all such laws as they should make, or at least such as they might impose upon us; in which course though they should intend our good, yet it might prove very prejudicial to us." This decision had not prevented friends in England from petitioning Parliament in favor of Massachusetts. As a result, that body issued an order "that we should enjoy all our liberties, etc., according to our patent, whereby our patent, which had been condemned and called in . . . was now implicitly revived and confirmed."

When civil war broke out, New England was predominantly on the side of Parliament. At the annual election in 1643, when the new officers were about to take the oath of allegiance, someone suggested that the King, by making war on Parliament, had forfeited the right to allegiance. It was thereupon agreed to omit any mention of him in the oath. Two years later when, as Winthrop put it, "some malignant spirits began to stir, and declare themselves for the king," the General Court cracked down with an order forbidding anyone to support the royalist cause by action, word, or writing.

By this time it was apparent that Parliament was coming out on top in the struggle. The order may even have been dictated by a desire to avoid giving offense to the winning side. For Winthrop, certainly, this was a guiding consideration. He shared in the general sympathy for the Parliamentary cause, but his caution grew as the gap between English and American Puritanism widened. He was eager to keep on the right side of Parliament, not only because Massachusetts might need its protection, but also because an aroused Parliament might attempt to impose its own religious schemes on Massachusetts. And Parliament's religious schemes could mean only two things: Presbyterianism, on the one hand, or toleration for heretical and erroneous doctrines, on the other.

In Rhode Island, Congregational Puritanism had developed along the same lines as in England, proliferating in a variety of opinions which were joined only by a belief in toleration. Besides the settlements made by Roger Williams and his followers at Providence and by Mrs. Hutchinson and hers on the island, there was now another south of Providence at Pawtuxet, led by Samuel Gorton, whose beliefs seemed even worse than those of his neighbors. None of the Rhode Islanders had any reason to love Massachusetts, and they were quick to see that things were going their way in England. They sent complaints and delegations to the mother country against the harsh and unfair treatment they consistently received from Massachusetts. Roger Williams was able to obtain a charter for his colony from Parliament, and he published in London attacks on the intolerance of Massachusetts. Letters that reached Boston from England cried shame upon Winthrop's regime for its harshness to dissenters, and Rhode Islanders returning home from the mother country landed triumphantly at Boston, bearing orders to let them pass in peace.

Within Massachusetts itself there was little sympathy

for the heresies prevailing around Narragansett Bay, and few persons were disposed to favor toleration as desirable in itself. But the population did include large numbers who might be susceptible to Presbyterianism. Those persons whom Congregationalism excluded from church membership were excluded not only from the sacraments and from a voice in the selection of their minister but also from the privileges of freemanship, the right to vote and hold office. Many nonmembers were good Puritans who would not have wanted the privileges of membership on any other terms than the existing laws required. But the group also included some less ardent souls, among them a few well-to-do merchants, who thought themselves entitled to a larger share in the management of the colony.

While Charles I had ruled undisputed, Massachusetts looked a much fairer place to live, even to nonmembers, than England. But with the ascendancy of the Long Parliament and of Presbyterianism in England, wealthy New England nonmembers could not fail to see how much larger their privileges would be in the mother country where property ownership would enable them to vote and hold office. They did not therefore return to England, but they did begin to think about the possibility of gaining the same privileges for themselves where they were.

By 1645 Winthrop and the other members of the General Court sensed their uneasiness and prepared to allay it; a bill drafted in the General Court extended the franchise to nonmembers in all town affairs. The bill also provided that certain nonmembers of large estate should be admitted to all the voting privileges of freemen. Unfortunately, before the bill could be passed, the expected storm fell upon the government.

The danger from the nonmembers had always lain not merely in a possible demand for the franchise, but rather in a demand for Presbyterianism. Under a Presbyterian organization there would have been no distinction between members and nonmembers. All would have been accepted into the church, and the religious basis for political rights would have been automatically removed.

It is impossible to say how much Presbyterian sentiment existed among the original settlers of Massachusetts, but there were certainly a few ministers who had never been wholly content with the Congregational organization. Possibly, too, the small number of immigrants who straggled in after 1640 brought some Presbyterian notions with them. It was, in any case, a newcomer to the colony who in 1646 attempted to organize the discontented in appealing to Parliament for a Presbyterian Massachusetts.

Robert Child was a doctor of medicine who first visited New England sometime between 1638 and 1641 and made the acquaintance of the leading men there, including John Winthrop's eldest son, John. After this visit he returned to England and witnessed the initial successes of Parliament. Most Englishmen on the Parliamentary side favored either Presbyterianism or toleration; Robert Child favored both. When he came back to New England in 1645, he was full of ideas for improving the place. He had thought of new crops that might be grown, new mines for lead and iron that might be developed—and a new way of organizing both church and state. In May 1645, he presented the General Court with a document entitled "Remonstrance and humble Petition," signed by himself and six friends who purported to speak for "divers others within this jurisdiction." No one will ever know how many others there were, but if discontent with either church or state in Massachusetts was at all wide, Child and his associates were giving it a chance for expression in an appeal to the rising power of Parliament.

That is what Child's remonstrance amounted to. Though in form a petition to the Massachusetts General Court, it was in fact a denunciation of the Congregational organization of churches, of the limitation of political rights to church members, and of the independence which Massachusetts claimed with regard to England. Child demanded closer dependence on the laws of England (and on the Parliament that made those laws), extension of political rights, and abandonment of the requirement of regenerate membership in the churches. Barring such an opening-up of church membership, he wished at least that dissenters from Congregationalism be allowed "to settle themselves here in a church way, according to the best reformations of England and Scotland."

The document was obviously prepared with a view to its rejection by the court. Written in a hortatory tone, it was directed more toward Presbyterians in old England than toward Congregationalists in New. It even contained the outright statement that if the demands were not carried out, the petitioners "shall be necessitated to apply our humble desires to the honourable houses of parliament, who we hope will take our sad conditions into their serious considerations."

If Winthrop had had his way, the government would not have risen to this bait. According to a later account, "an eminent person," presumably Winthrop, held a private conference with the remonstrants during the summer of 1646, but to no effect. Even so, Winthrop hoped that the dispute would die of inanition. As he put it later to his son, "I had thought we should onely have declared our apprehensions concerning the Petition, without questioning the Petitioners, but the deputyes called upon it." As usual it was the deputies who insisted on a showdown, and once the petitioners appeared in court, the possibility of a quiet ending was over. In the petition they had threatened an appeal to Parliament; before the court, Child announced that they had acted beneath themselves in ever presenting the petition, that they should have proceeded directly to the authorities in England, and that this was what they would now do.

Here was an open challenge that Winthrop could not ignore. Child, with his truculent assurance, was appealing before the court had even considered his case. What he wanted, apparently, was to draw the attention of Parliament to the fact that Massachusetts was going her own way, flouting the terms of her charter, the laws of England, and the power of Parliament. If Child were successful, Parliament might be aroused to assert its new authority and reduce the colony to submission and to Presbyterianism. From here on Winthrop fought, as he had fought Anne Hutchinson, by fair means and foul. Child and the other petitioners were fined for contempt of court and sedition, Child's fine being fifty pounds, and Winthrop told them that no appeal to higher authority in England would be recognized. While Child and the other remonstrants prepared to depart for England and see about that, Winthrop waited. When they were ready to embark, he seized them again. In one of their trunks he found two more incriminating petitions addressed to the authorities in England, one signed by twenty-five nonfreemen, calling for liberty of conscience, the other signed by the original six remonstrants, calling for the establishment of Presbyterianism. Both petitions asked for closer control of the government by England.

Once again Child and his friends were indicted for sedition, and they were held until the following spring (1647) before they were tried. In the interval the General Court shipped off dispatches to England, explaining the whole affair in somewhat different terms from those Child might have been expected to use; and Winthrop pulled every wire he could. By the time the remonstrants were tried again, fined again, and allowed to depart, Parliament had been persuaded that Massachusetts was in good hands. A Parliamentary commission had issued a statement confirming the General Court's jurisdiction "with all that freedom and latitude that may, in any respect, be duly claimed by you." When Child arrived in England, he found he was too late to win there what he had lost in Massachusetts. Presbyterianism was already on the decline; Oliver Cromwell was on the rise; and that old New Englander, Hugh Peter, was taking a large hand in public affairs.

Winthrop had won again. The Child affair was the greatest challenge his colony ever faced from foreign intervention. The challenge had been met and met with a reassuring unanimity: Child had been able to persuade only twenty-five nonfreemen to sign his petition in their behalf. Winthrop could rejoice in victory without knowing that it might eventually prove a victory for isolationism. For the moment the important thing was to preserve the liberty of Massachusetts to carry out her commission, and in this he had succeeded, just as he had succeeded against Roger Williams and Anne Hutchinson. How his success would be used by the next generation was a matter he could not control.

After his death the colony did use its independence to become more and more provincial, more and more tribal, more and more isolationist; but the broader vision that Winthrop stood for could never be wholly subdued. No Puritan could be a Puritan and remain untouched by it, for it arose out of the central Puritan dilemma, the problem of doing right in a world that does wrong. Winthrop was not the last Puritan—or the last American—to wrestle with the problem or to reach an answer. There would be other men like him to open up the horizons when they became clouded by zeal or indifference.

With Child disposed of, the General Court resumed consideration of its plan to extend voting privileges and granted to nonfreemen a voice in the choice of town officers (but not of deputies to the General Court). This was the only concession thought necessary. The Massachusetts system was now as completely worked out as it was ever likely to be. A new code of laws, incorporating Nathaniel Ward's Body of Liberties along with other important acts of the General Court, was published in 1648, and in the same year the ministers of all the New England churches, meeting in a synod, produced a document defining the standard organization and procedures of the Congregational churches. If the world wished a model of the society which God ordained for men in church and state, here it was, articulate, precise, and certain. And here were men and women living it.

As far as Winthrop could tell, they might continue to live it in the future. That the rest of the world was not hastening to imitate them did not surprise him. When God was ready to save the world, evil would everywhere be brought under control, but not before. Meanwhile one could rejoice to live in Massachusetts. Winthrop felt relieved when the General Court decided not to send him to England to counter the expected attack there by Child. The court decided against it because they were afraid he might be drawn into Parliament and so be lost to them. Winthrop would doubtless have gone if they had asked him, but he was happier to stay at home, in the good land he had grown to love.

He was nearer the end than he knew. In the summer of 1647 Margaret died, "a woman," he noted quietly in his journal, "of singular virtue, prudence, modesty, and piety and specially beloved and honored of all the country." He had loved her with a warmth that glows in every line he ever addressed to her. But they both had learned long since that this world was for the living, and to go through it in mourning was to dishonor the God who had made it. By the time Winthrop was chosen governor once more the following spring he had married again—a Charlestown widow named Martha Coytmore. Before the year was out she presented him with another son.

He was sixty now, and he kept a tenacious hold on life.

Though ill for six weeks with a fever in the summer of 1648, he was abroad and at his business every day—the business of living in Massachusetts. In his journal, as always, he set down the homely details: the scarcity of corn (because so much had been sent in trade to the West Indies and the Azores), the abundance of passenger pigeons, a plague of brown flies ("about the bigness of the top of a man's little finger"), the burning of a barn at Salem, the discovery of a new path to Connecticut, the drowning of five persons who ventured out on thin ice in the winter of 1648–1649. This was life in Massachusetts—and death. In February he went to bed with a feverish distemper and a cough. On March 26 he reached what in life he had never sought, a separation from his sinful fellow men.

Acknowledgments and Sources

I began the study of Puritanism sixty years ago under the tutelage of Perry Miller and Samuel Eliot Morison. If I have contributed anything toward the understanding of New England Puritanism, it is because of the stimulation and encouragement I received from them and their writings.

In the preparation of this book I acquired more immediate debts. Professor Donald Fleming read the next to last draft in its entirety and offered valuable suggestions, most of which have been adopted to the great improvement of the text. My wife, the late Helen M. Morgan, worked with me at every stage. Her editorial and critical discernment, exercised on innumerable drafts, is responsible for whatever final clarity of language the book may possess.

I have not supported my views by footnote citations, but the sources for this period are well-known. Chief among them, for purposes of this study, were the surviving papers of John Winthrop and of other members of the Winthrop family. Most of these have been published by the Massachusetts Historical Society, first in scattered volumes of its *Collections,* and subsequently in a comprehensive edition, arranged chronologically (*Winthrop Papers,* 1929–). This edition, still in progress, is a model of editorial scholarship. The first five volumes, beginning with the earliest family papers from England, reach to the year 1649, the year of John Winthrop's death. The journal

Winthrop kept from the time of his departure for New England is now available in a definitive edition, *The Journal of John Winthrop, 1630–1649,* Richard Dunn, James Savage, and Laetitia Yeandle, eds. (1996).

Other original sources of value have been the *Records of the Governor and Company of the Massachusetts Bay* (N. B. Shurtleff, ed., 5 volumes in 6. Boston, 1853–1854); the various compilations of seventeenth-century Massachusetts laws (Max Farrand, ed., *The Laws and Liberties of Massachusetts.* Cambridge, Mass., 1929; W. H. Whitmore, ed., *The Colonial Laws of Massachusetts.* Boston, 1889); and the writings and papers of other early settlers scattered through the following publications: the *Collections* and *Proceedings* of the Massachusetts Historical Society, the *Publications* of the Colonial Society of Massachusetts, the *Proceedings* of the American Antiquarian Society, the *Publications* of the Narragansett Club, the *Publications* of the Prince Society, the *New England Quarterly,* Alexander Young's *Chronicles of the First Planters of the Colony of Massachusetts-Bay* (Boston, 1846), and Thomas Hutchinson's *Collection of Original Papers Relative to the History of the Colony of Massachusetts-Bay* (Boston, 1769).

Most of the quotations in the text are from the *Winthrop Papers* or from Winthrop's *Journal.* In transcribing them I have modernized the spelling by expanding abbreviations and by substituting *j* for *i* and *v* for *u* and vice versa, wherever appropriate. I have also written *than* instead of *then* and *own* instead of *one* where these meanings were clearly intended. Otherwise I have followed the original spelling, which in the seventeenth century had not yet been standardized.

Secondary Works

Modern study of early New England and its founders began with Miller and Morison, and their works remain the starting point for historians like myself who have followed in their wake. The crucial titles are Morison: *Builders of the Bay Colony* (1930), *The Founding of Harvard College* (1935), *Harvard College in the Seventeenth Century* (1936); Miller: *Orthodoxy in Massachusetts* (1933), *The New England Mind: The Seventeenth Century* (1939), *The New England Mind: From Colony to Province* (1953). Subsequent works which have reassessed Miller's grand synthesis, in whole or in part, include Robert Middlekauff, *The Mathers* (1971); David D. Hall, *The Faithful Shepherd* (1972); Harry Stout, *The New England Soul* (1986); and Stephen Foster, *The Long Argument* (1991). In the following paragraphs I have tried to list some of the more important works, both old and new, that bear on the topics and events treated in particular chapters.

CHAPTERS I AND II. The social and economic background of late sixteenth-century and early seventeenth-century England is treated in Wallace Notestein, *The English People on the Eve of Colonization* (1954); Carl Bridenbaugh, *Vexed and Troubled Englishmen* (1968); Lawrence Stone, *The Crisis of the Aristocracy* (1965); and *The Agrarian History of England and Wales,* volume IV, Joan Thirsk, ed. (1967). The political developments of the time are a subject of dispute among historians. The seminal works are J. E. Neale, *The Elizabethan House of Commons* (1949) and *Elizabeth I and her Parliaments* (1953). A revisionist view of the role of Parliament is Conrad Russell, *Parliaments and English Politics, 1621–1629* (1979), to which may be compared Lawrence Stone, *The Causes of the English Revolution, 1529–1642* (1972). On the development of Puritanism in England the standard works now, apart from Miller, are Patrick Collinson, *The Elizabethan Puritan Movement* (1967), and Foster's *The Long Argument,* but William Haller, *The Rise of Puritanism* (1938), is still useful. Charles Cohen, *God's Caress*

(1986), offers a searching analysis of Puritan psychology, with a good deal of attention to Winthrop.

CHAPTERS III AND IV. These chapters are based almost entirely on *Winthrop Papers*.

CHAPTER V. The "great migration" to New England has been treated from different perspectives in many recent books, most directly in David Cressy, *Coming Over* (1987), and Virginia DeJohn Anderson, *New England's Generation* (1991). Francis Jennings sees it from the perspective of the Indians in *The Invasion of America* (1975). A more dispassionate discussion of the interaction between English and Indians is Neal Salisbury, *Manitou and Providence* (1982). William Cronon discusses the ecological consequences in *Changes in the Land* (1983).

CHAPTER VI. The sense of mission felt by the Massachusetts Puritans is emphasized by Perry Miller in *The New England Mind: the Seventeenth Century* and in *Errand into the Wilderness* (1956). On the role of the family see my *The Puritan Family* (revised ed., 1966) and John Demos, *A Little Commonwealth* (1970). The organization of Congregational churches is discussed in all the general works on Puritanism and more specifically in Ola Winslow, *Meetinghouse Hill* (1952), and my *Visible Saints* (1963).

CHAPTERS VII AND VIII. The story of the establishment of the Massachusetts government in the first four years is told in every account of early New England. I have collected all the surviving sources along with the differing interpretations of them by four different historians in *The Founding of Massachusetts* (1964).

CHAPTER IX. I have offered a more extensive interpretation of Roger Williams in *Roger Williams: The Church and the State* (1967). The best biography is Ola Winslow, *Master Roger Williams* (1957). Philip Gura, *A Glimpse of Sion's Glory* (1984), gives a more general view of radical separatism.

CHAPTER X. All the relevant documents in the case of Anne Hutchinson have been collected with an important introduction and notes in David D. Hall, *The Antinomian Controversy, 1636–1638* (1968). Norman Pettit, *The Heart Prepared* (1966), and William Stoever, *A Faire and Easie Way to Heaven* (1978), discuss some of the theological issues. Emory Battis, *Saints and Sectaries* (1962), analyzes the social composition of Hutchinson's supporters.

CHAPTER XI. The best studies of the development of Massachusetts law in these years are George Haskins, *Law and Authority in Early Massachusetts* (1960), and David Konig, *Law and Society in Puritan Massachusetts* (1979). Alfred Cave, *The Pequot War* (1996), offers a balanced account. I have given a more extended discussion of church–state relations in *Roger Williams*. Robert Wall, *Massachusetts Bay: The Crucial Decade, 1640–1650* (1972), focuses on the conflict between magistrates and deputies.

The origins and organization of the seventeenth-century New England town have been more closely examined in recent decades than ever before. Among the most significant works are Sumner Powell, *Puritan Village* (1963); Darrett Rutman, *Winthrop's Boston* (1965); Kenneth Lockridge, *A New England Town* (1970); Philip Greven, *Four Generations* (1970); David Allen, *In English Ways* (1981); Stephen Innes, *Labor in a New Land* (1983); and John Martin, *Profits in the Wilderness* (1991).

CHAPTER XII. The problem I have tried to handle in this chapter forms the theme of the title essay in Miller, *Errand into the Wilderness*. Middlekauff, *The Mathers*, offers a different view. Raymond Stearns, *The Strenuous Puritan: Hugh Peter* (1954), deals with a leading Puritan who returned to England. Cressy, *Coming Over*, also discusses the return migration. Bernard Bailyn, *The New England Merchants in the Seventeenth Century* (1955), analyzes economic developments.

CHAPTER XIII. This chapter is based entirely on Winthrop's *Journal* and the *Winthrop Papers*. I know of no modern books devoted to the relations of Massachusetts with England or Canada during this period.

Index

Note: John Winthrop is abbreviated JW.